December King

December King

nald Douglas Smith

© Copyright 1983 • Broadman Press
All rights reserved.

4245-16
ISBN: 0-8054-4516-1

Dewey Decimal Classification: F
Library of Congress Catalog Card Number: 82-70368

Printed in the United States of America

To my Lord,
my parents, my big brother,
Lisa, Heidi, and Beau.
I love you.

Contents

1. The Boat 7
2. A New Look 11
3. Plans Are Made 15
4. The Move 22
5. New Country 27
6. First Fish 31
7. The Outsider 38
8. Chautauqua 48
9. Loneliness 62
10. December King 72
11. Home Sweet Home 86

December King

1
The Boat

A good twenty feet long, a boat lay hull up on a vacant lot surrounded by overgrown eucalyptus trees. It looked like the kind of boat dreams are made of: crude, weatherbeaten, and abandoned—or so it seemed. Peter's dad saw it first and pointed it out. Peter could hardly sit still as his dad eased the family pickup over to the curb. Peter was out inspecting every inch of the hull before his dad was around the truck. "It looks great, Dad!"

Jim Miles was no stranger to youthful enthusiasm. His son had plenty to spare. Jim had only reluctantly learned to control his own as he had grown up, taking on the responsibilities of a man. He too thought that the boat was a great find. Still, he dared not show too much excitement because he did not want his son to build false hopes. He did not even know if the boat could be had.

The paint on the hull was cracked and peeling. The inside could not be seen because the boat lay upside down on the ground. Aside from the obvious fact that it had fallen into neglect, Jim noted that it was well built.

Looking about, Jim saw a crude sign on a shack beyond the eucalyptus trees. A dump truck and a small tractor with a scoop were parked behind the shack. A lot of junk lay piled around the area. "Come on, Peter, let's see who owns it," he suggested.

As the two neared the shack, the leaves under a nearby eucalyptus rustled. Snarling and growling, his fangs bared, a ferocious hound came charging at the innocent trespassers. Jim grabbed his son and jumped in front of him. Peter's eyes got very large, and he was about to yell when the hound reached the end of his chain.

"He won't hurt you," called a gruff voice. The hound quit growling and slowly retreated to the shade of his tree.

As they turned around, the boy and his dad were confronted by a rough-looking man fully as wide at the belt as the door of the shack through which he came. The man wore baggy trousers, soiled and greasy; a tee shirt with no sleeves and many holes; and a frayed straw hat. He had a tattoo on his arm and a cigar in his mouth.

"Who owns that old boat?" asked Jim, accepting the stranger's character witness for the hound.

"Well, I do—sorta," snorted the round man.

"Sort of?"

"Well, she once belonged to Willard Topping, my best friend; but he won't be usin' it no more—he died."

"I'm sorry," Jim said sincerely.

"Oh, he had a good life. He built that old boat himself. Built her for some movie outfit—MGB or somethin'. He took a bunch of cameramen and their gear down the Colorado to film some movie. Never used her much after that. Now she just sits there and reminds me of him. You want her?"

"Well," said Jim, as Peter's eyes lit up, "I might. How much do you want for her?"

The man's gaze shifted to the boat, which he could see through the trees. He bit down on his cigar, while he thought for a minute. "Give me thirty bucks for old Willard's widow and she's yours," he said, casually.

Peter stared at his father with his mouth open, waiting for his reply.

"That's a good price and more than fair. My only concern is how to get her home," said Jim.

"Do you live far?"

"About a mile."

"Well, that's no problem," reassured the man, "I have a truck

The Boat

out back, and I would be glad to haul her to your house. Besides, from the look on your boy's face there, the old boat has found a good home."

Peter could scarcely believe his ears. A boat. A big boat. Built for the movies. "Wow!" He let out a yell and ran to the boat. Slapping her sides with his hand, he danced around her smiling. "Wait 'til Mom sees her!" he shouted.

Jim was pleased, too, but he was not quite as excited about Peter's mother seeing the boat. He knew the boat needed a lot of work. Still, he knew that Nancy Miles would be pleased when the old boat was all fixed up.

The boat was sturdily built and quite heavy. After some time, they finally got her loaded onto the dump truck. Tony (which was what the fat man said to call him) used the tractor with a rope tied to the scoop to hoist the bow end up onto the truck. Then he got behind the boat with the scoop and pushed it into the truck bed.

When they got home, Jim jumped out of the pickup and directed Tony as he backed the dump truck into the driveway. As Peter looked on, his dad and Tony raised the bed of the dump truck to a slight angle. Loosening the rope that tied the boat to the truck bed, they slid the old boat down onto the cement.

In no time at all, Jim had her propped up on some blocks, still upside down, and Tony was saying good-bye and good sailing. It was then that Peter's mother stepped out the side door with a look of surprise on her face and stood staring at the old boat. Upside down the boat looked like a beached whale.

"Well," said Jim, "what do you think?"

"It's big," Nancy replied, her eyes wide to take it all in.

It was a glorious boat to Peter, and he ran to hug his mother in his excitement. Nancy was pleased by her son's joy. She had long ago learned that she could trust Jim's instincts about such things. Therefore, she did not say anything that might spoil Peter's and his father's enthusiasm, although she thought that the boat surely looked "old." The old boat had certainly found a home.

Jim and Peter stood admiring the new addition to the family, when Nancy suddenly said, "I've got it."

"Got what?" Jim inquired.

"A name. Every boat has to have a name."

"What is it, Mom?" Peter asked, excitedly.

"Kitty Clyde's Sister," his mother answered.

Nancy always was a little unpredictable, and that was the strangest name for a boat that Peter or his dad had ever heard. As they looked at each other, then at the boat, and then back at each other, they started to laugh. It was a perfect name for the old riverboat.

2
A New Look

Kitty Clyde's Sister had come to rest in the Miles's driveway in the last weeks of winter. Peter was in school. He spent many days in the house after school, gazing out at the old boat through drizzling rain. He had to help his mother on these days by watching Anne, his little sister. Anne was so little that watching her could truly be a chore. That meant that he had to take her by the hand or pick her up all the time to keep her out of mischief. Sometimes Nancy made cookies or popcorn to make the time pass more pleasantly. Still, all that time spent in the house made Peter long for the outdoors.

It was not so bad when Jim came home from work because he made drawings of how the old boat would be fixed up when the weather turned warmer. That was fun for Peter. He often dreamed about the boat in his sleep. Each time, when he dreamed, *Kitty Clyde's Sister* looked better and better—just as his father's plans were shaping up.

When Jim sat down at the kitchen table with his son to make plans for their boat, he was almost as excited as Peter was. To Jim, *Kitty Clyde's Sister* was more than just a boat. It was the only real evidence of the new life which Jim was planning for his family. The city was a good place to make a living, and Jim was pleased with his job. Nevertheless, he had known the beauty and the peace that existed outside the city.

Each year, the Miles family took a two week vacation trip north of the big city. They were all in love with a particular river and the country surrounding it far to the north. Now Jim was planning a new future for the old boat and a new home for his family at the same time. Peter was not aware of all these plans. It was enough for him to share in the plans for the fixing up of the old boat.

At long last the rain stopped coming, and the days became warmer. Little Anne could play outside in the backyard, and Peter did not have to pay such close attention to what she was up to. When Peter came home from school, he hurried to get his homework done. Then he did whatever chores his mother might have for him. He wanted to be all done in time to help his dad with the work on *Kitty Clyde's Sister* when he came home from his job.

Each afternoon when Jim came home there was quite a commotion. He would say hello to Nancy and pick Anne up to give her a squeeze as he came through the front door. All the while, Peter would be urging his father to hurry out to the boat before the daylight was gone. Jim was not hard to hurry because he enjoyed working on the boat as much as Peter did.

When the old boat came to the Miles's house, it was not much to look at. The paint was cracked and peeling on the hull. The planks which formed the seats were split. There was weather-ruined plywood everywhere on the inside. Still, she had many good points.

The frame of the old boat was made of heavy timbers. She was a good twenty feet from bow to stern. The steering mechanism, which was designed to attach to dual outboard motors, was intact. There was only one small patch of bad wood in the hull. Most important, the entire boat was firmly held together by hundreds of brass wood screws.

Peter and his dad made many repairs and changes. The hull was scraped and sanded smooth. The small patch of bad wood was removed with a hammer and a chisel. A fresh piece was cut and sealed into place. Then, one weekend, the primer coat of marine paint was applied. The following Saturday a final coat of paint went on. Jim chose blue for the bottom of the boat. He told Peter that blue was best because fish would not see the boat as easily against the blue of the sky above.

A New Look

It was a big day when the old boat was finally turned upright. Now they could begin work on the inside. Peter admired his father's skill as he watched him repair the old boat. Each afternoon an old piece of plywood was removed and a new piece went into place. As each day came to an end, the sun's light was fading on the old boat. Peter stood beside his dad and happily admired the handiwork of the day. He hardly spoke of anything besides the old boat to his friends at school.

One day Jim came home from work with great news. "I found a trailer for *Kitty Clyde's Sister!*" he announced. The used trailer lay under a load of discarded wood beside a house near Jim's work. The owner had almost forgotten about the trailer, and Jim was able to buy it for only fifty dollars.

Two new tires were purchased for the trailer. A change or two was made in the frame. The pickup truck was fitted with a trailer hitch. Now they could get the old boat to water.

Some Saturdays were spent gathering parts from here and there for the boat. An old ship's wheel—not too large—was just right for *Kitty Clyde's Sister*. Brass railing and a brass bell to give her some class were purchased. An anchor and an anchor rope, with a pulley mounted on a boom, were acquired.

Jim planned to build a small cabin on the boat. Accordingly, a brass lamp and two round portholes were bought to give light in the cabin. A round wooden table was designed to collapse and form a bed with its bench seats, when not in use. This was to be the only furnishing in the small cabin.

Soon the cabin was built, and the new wood was varnished. All that remained were the finishing touches. Two new motors were purchased. By now the old boat looked like a new boat, and the money spent on the brand-new motors did not seem like too much.

Finally, the boat was ready. Nancy put on the final touch, painting *Kitty Clyde's Sister* across the stern. Then the whole Miles family stood back and admired their fine, new boat. Peter and his dad smiled as they beheld the results of all their hard work. Nancy was proud of them, and she was proud to be the one to name their boat. Anne was too little to know why she was happy, but she was happy also.

3
Plans Are Made

School was out for summer vacation, and Peter was home every day now. Jim came home from work one evening and gathered the family around the kitchen table. Peter could see that his dad was very excited about something. He was anxious to know what it was.

"I have made arrangements to take my two weeks of vacation next month," began Jim.

That was enough for Peter, and he shouted, "Oh, boy!"

The whole family looked forward to these yearly vacations because they always went on a trip to the river up north to camp and fish. From the time they started packing for each trip until the day they returned home, it was one big adventure every year. No one was more excited about this news than Peter. But there was more.

"This time we will be looking for a place to live, and I will look for work while we are at the river," Jim continued.

Nancy's eyes shone with excitement, and Peter could scarcely believe his ears. "Wow!" he exclaimed. "You mean we're going to move to the river, Dad?"

Jim explained that if he could find work and a suitable place to live, they would come home and sell the house as soon as possible. Then they would be off to a new home near the river that they all loved so dearly.

Little Anne did not understand what was being said, but she could feel the excitement in the room. She began to giggle, and that made everyone laugh with joy. It was a very merry evening.

Peter had many questions about how soon they might move, where they might live on the river, and all sorts of things. He could scarcely go to sleep that night, as he thought of this wonderful new adventure. It seemed that this adventure would never end. Peter was sad when he thought of leaving all his friends at school and near home. But he was too excited about the move to be sad for long.

The month before their trip seemed to pass slowly for the Miles family. Finally the evening came when Jim came home from work and told Peter that it was time to pack the truck and hitch up *Kitty Clyde's Sister* for the trip. They would leave early in the morning of the next day, Saturday. While Nancy made sandwiches to eat on the road, Jim and Peter loaded the camping gear into the back of the truck and hitched up their wonderful boat.

Peter felt as though he would burst from the excitement, as they made final preparations for the trip. He scarcely slept a wink that night. When his dad came in to wake him in the morning, he was dressed and ready to go, having heard the alarm clock go off in his parents' room across the hall.

The trip north was a bit slower than usual. For the first time, the Miles family towed a boat behind their pickup truck on their vacation. Peter didn't mind at all. It was a good feeling to look out the back window and see *Kitty Clyde's Sister* bouncing along behind. It almost looked as though she were in the water already, being bounced by the waves.

Peter fell asleep on his father's shoulder as they drove. He had a smile on his face. He dreamed of riding in the boat at the mouth of the river, fishing, and hearing the seagulls, with the salt spray all around.

When Peter awoke, the sun was low in the sky. Jim told him that they were only an hour away from the river. They each ate a sandwich as they drove along. Everyone was hungry which made the sandwiches taste extra good.

When the sun was hanging just over the hills to the left, the Miles family rounded a bend in the highway. Just ahead and below them was their destination. They could see the small community at the mouth of the river. It nestled among the rolling hills on both

Plans Are Made

sides of the river. They could also see where the highway crossed the river over a bridge with low cement walls.

The river was wide where it entered the ocean. By now the sun was just above the sea to the west. A silver path stretched to the horizon as they crossed the bridge. The hills to the east were covered with large pine trees. The long shadows of the tall trees had darkened the hills, making them look cold and mysterious.

Upon crossing the bridge, Jim turned the pickup, followed by *Kitty Clyde's Sister,* onto the road running along the north side of the river. They would camp in a small campground about six miles upriver. The campground was owned and operated by the Bobos.

June and Bruce Bobo were happy to see the Miles family again. Each summer the Bobos extended their hospitality to the Mileses as though they were close relatives. The Bobos were friendly people by nature, and they had known the Miles family since Peter was a baby.

This year the same spot near the river was reserved for Jim and his family, as in years past. While Jim, Bruce, and Peter set up the tent, they chatted about many things. Little Anne was getting prettier. Peter must have grown a foot. What a fine boat *Kitty Clyde's Sister* was. And on and on.

June helped Nancy set up the outdoor kitchen. They too kept up a lively conversation.

Finally the camp was in order, and all gathered around the camp fire to talk and rekindle their warm friendship. When Peter and Anne went to bed in the tent that night, they were soon lulled to sleep by the happy sounds. There were the adults' conversation around the crackling camp fire and the quiet throb of the river, as it passed the campsite on its way to the ocean.

The next day, Peter was up with the sun. Warm rays of light streamed through the open tent flaps. Down to his old friend, the river, he ran.

At the campground, the river made a wide bend. It ran deep and slow for a hundred feet. Then it narrowed to pass swiftly between a high, sheer cliff on the south side and a sloping hill to the north. That stretch of river was called "the chutes." It was a great place to fish because the steelhead trout (and salmon when they were running) would pause in the slow water at the head of the chutes after their hard swim through the swift rapids.

Peter gathered several smooth, flat stones to skip on the mirror-like surface of the deep water. He stood on one of the boat docks and hurled one rock after another, pausing only to watch each one bounce and skitter across the water. What a thrill it would be to live here and to be greeted every morning by his friend the river.

That day, after breakfast, Jim backed the trailer to the water and launched *Kitty Clyde's Sister*. Peter and Nancy cheered and Anne giggled. The old boat looked grand in the water. She fit right into her new surroundings.

The two weeks spent at the river were full of excitement and fun. Days were spent fishing, swimming, and riding in *Kitty Clyde's Sister*. The salmon were not running at this time of the year, but steelheads were abundant in the river. The Miles family caught their share. Several evenings Nancy cooked enough so that the Bobos could join them for dinner. After dinner the evenings were spent around a camp fire, or they all went up to the lodge.

The lodge was one of the Bobo's campground facilities. The old-timers gathered around a huge stone fireplace to tell fish stories. The lodge also served as a small store in which groceries, cold drinks, and fishing supplies could be purchased.

Peter enjoyed the time spent at the lodge, which was built of rough logs. A big, old parrot sat on his perch in one corner and swayed from side to side. He talked quite well and took sunflower seeds out of Peter's fingers. He said "Hello," "Where's the fish?" "That's a fish story," and many other things. Sometimes he said something funny at just the right time—when some fisherman had just finished a story about the one that got away. Then everyone roared with laughter.

Trophy fish of great sizes and antlers from deer and elk hung on the walls around the room. There were plenty of comfortable,

Plans Are Made 19

wooden chairs with thick cushions between broad, flat arms. The campers gathered them in a circle in front of the fireplace and settled into them.

June made popcorn over the fire in a metal popcorn shaker some evenings. Peter had never tasted better popcorn. After a while, when the conversation tapered off, the only sounds were the crackling of the warm fire and the tick-tock of an old clock on the heavy oak mantel.

Each day Jim looked in the local newspaper for a job and a place to live. He talked with Bruce about their plans to move to the river as well. But Jim had no success. There just weren't any job openings. That was a great disappointment to all because the plans to move to the river depended upon Jim being able to find work there. The situation was beginning to look hopeless until the evening before the Miles family was to leave.

Bruce came down to the campsite. He told Jim that he had an idea which he wanted to discuss. The two men sat down at the picnic table near the camp fire. Nancy brought them each a cup of coffee and went back to washing the dinner dishes in a pan of hot water. Peter had finished clearing the table, and he sat down to listen.

Bruce knew what a hard thing it was for Jim to have to give up his dream of moving to the river. He could sense the disappointment that Peter felt also.

It had not always been easy for Bruce to provide for June and himself, and they didn't have children as Jim did. Before they bought the trailer court with the campground and the lodge, Bruce had found it necessary to work several jobs. He worked for farmers and ranchers in the surrounding countryside during the winter months, doing whatever odd jobs he could find. During the warmer months many tourists visited the river. Bruce piloted a riverboat, carrying tourists up river about ten miles to an old farmhouse where they received a farm-fresh home-cooked meal.

The riverboat rides started before the river road went in. The mail was delivered to the residents up river by motor boat. The mail boat ride was continued as a tourist attraction after the road was built. The meal which the tourists received consisted of fresh, country-fried chicken; milk straight from the cow; churned butter; corn on the cob just off the stalk; mashed potatoes with gravy; homemade rolls with homemade blackberry preserves; and for dessert, blackberry pie made from fresh-picked berries with homemade ice cream.

After their meal, Bruce ferried the tourists back downriver to their cars. The boat was stopped along the way to allow the tourists to watch fishermen land their fish. They could photograph wildlife along the river also. They saw bear, deer, and many other animals. The Miles family went on one of these boat rides with Bruce, and they loved it. Even though the Bobos owned and operated the trailer court, Bruce had to pilot one of these mail boats to help make ends meet. But that was not what Bruce came to talk to Jim about.

It seemed that a friend of Bruce's was moving out of the area. He had a business and a house for sale. Jim had never owned his own business. He had always worked for someone else. Nevertheless, he was willing to listen to anything at that point.

"It's a boat rental place," Bruce explained, "complete with a tackle shop and a small cafe. And there's a house with three bedrooms directly across the highway from the business."

Peter thought that this all sounded great. To everyone's surprise, so did his dad. Jim even surprised himself because he was not worried about whether he would be successful. He knew that he could succeed. He couldn't help it with such a wonderful business in such a wonderful place.

Early the next day, which was Saturday, Bruce took Jim and his family to the mouth of the river where the boat rental docks were. Bruce introduced Jim to his friend, who was an older man named Jake.

"Everybody calls me Dutchman," said Jake, "because I named my business "The Dutchman's—Boats, Tackle, Food."

The boats, the docks, and the buildings were in good condition.

Plans Are Made

Everything was even better than Jim had hoped it would be. Dutchman was a fair man, and Jim thought his price was reasonable. Nancy loved the house which sat upon the hill across the highway and faced out to sea. She was already thinking up a menu for the small cafe.

Peter was too busy inspecting the boats and the docks to pay any attention to the business talk. Jim made an agreement with Dutchman. Jim would sell his house, make a down payment on Jake's house and business, and pay so much per month until the balance could be paid off.

The rest of the day was spent packing the truck and hitching up *Kitty Clyde's Sister* for the drive home. Now they would get home late on Sunday instead of Saturday, and Jim would have to unpack in the dark. That didn't matter though. Jim's excitement was only exceeded by that of his son. The whole family seemed to be ready to burst with joy as they drove home that Sunday.

As they laughed and talked of their new home and their wonderful new business, Nancy did it again. "I've got it," she said.

"What?" asked Peter.

"The name," she replied. "Every business has to have a name."

"What? What?" Peter and his dad echoed.

"Best Place for Miles."

4
The Move

The Miles family returned from their vacation in late July. Peter was still out of school. Now that plans had been made to move to the river, Peter found his days full of activity. It was clear to him that the sooner the house was sold, the sooner they could move.

There were many things that needed to be done to help sell the house. Jim had to go to work each day, which meant he could only work on the house in the evenings and on weekends. He found that he could show Peter what to do. Then, while Jim was at work, Peter would work very hard on whatever needed to be done. Jim was amazed at the energy and ambition that Peter showed.

The grass was mowed and edged twice a week. With a little extra watering, the yard soon began to look like a carefully tended park. The eaves and the wood trim were scraped and painted. The windows were washed inside and out, and the screens were cleaned. The walls and the woodwork in the house were scrubbed, and the furniture was put in order.

By the time school started again in September, the Mileses were ready to sell their house. A sign went up in the front yard. Before the first week passed, the house was sold. The man who bought the house said that he had driven by every day on his way to work. He had watched the cleanup work progressing, and he had wondered if the house would be up for sale. When the sign went up, he had brought his wife over. The house was just what they had been looking for.

All that remained was to pack for the move and to bid farewell to friends and family in the area. Bruce Bobo had written to Jim to

The Move

assure him that Dutchman was patiently waiting for him to sell the house. Bruce was happy when Jim called on the telephone to announce the sale. He said he would go right over to Dutchman's place and give him the good news.

It was arranged for the Miles family to move in on the first of October or whenever they could get there after that. The weather would start to get chilly soon, and Bruce urged Jim to get there as soon as possible.

Peter was excited about the move. Nevertheless, he felt some sadness as he said good-bye to his friends at school. They were all excited for him, and they made him promise to write to them. Some of his close friends said that they would try to talk their parents into going to the river for their vacations the following summer.

Loading all their belongings into the rented moving truck was no easy task for the Miles family. A couple of pieces of furniture and a lot of miscellaneous items in the garage had to be sold in a yard sale or given away. Jim worked hard all through the month of September to get everything ready for the move. He was home every day for the last week, having left his job. Finally, the day of departure arrived.

Peter was amazed at all the stuff that was being moved. The rented truck was full of furniture, dishes, boxes of books, and much, much more. Jim would drive that truck, and Peter was to ride with him. Then there was the pickup truck, which was full of boxes. Bringing up the rear of the caravan was *Kitty Clyde's Sister*. She, too, was loaded with boxes and things from the garage—as much as the pickup could pull. Nancy would drive the pickup and Anne would ride with her.

Peter felt strange when he looked over his shoulder at his old house one last time. As the big truck pulled away, he felt as though he were saying good-bye to an old friend. That house would always be the scene of his childhood, and Peter would carry many fond memories of those years for the rest of his life.

Now began a new chapter in Peter's life. "What new experience will be mine in my new home? What new friends will I find? Will I fit in at my new school?" These were some of the questions that kept Peter's mind occupied as Jim drove the moving truck north.

The trip was uneventful. Everything arrived in one piece, and nothing was left behind. The new house was empty and ready for its new owners to move in. Nancy was pleased with how clean Dutchman's wife had left everything.

The Miles family arrived at their new home on Saturday night. Peter would be enrolled in the school across the bridge on the south side of the bay on Monday. Sunday was to be the only full day for him to get a look at his new surroundings. After a good meal in their new home and a brief evening around a fire in the fireplace, Peter was off to bed.

When he awoke in his new room, which was empty except for his sleeping bag (all the furniture was still in the moving truck), Peter was greeted by warm rays of sunlight pouring through the windows. He was also aware of a new sound. Somewhere nearby several roosters were crowing at the new day. What a change from the old house! Peter loved it. He was up, dressed, and out of the house before anyone else was stirring.

Peter's new home, an old, two-story house, sat on a hill overlooking the bay. There were large pine trees on the slope behind the house. A stack of firewood at least ten feet long and four feet high filled the space between two tree trunks at the side of the house. On a limb jutting out from the far tree hung a swing, put there by Dutchman for his son.

Peter climbed into the seat and was soon swinging far out over the slope. "Wow!" could he see from there! At the top of his swinging path, he could see up the river for at least a mile and out to sea for what seemed to be several miles. He could see boats sliding over the rolling waves. Peter learned later that these were the few boats operated by the commercial fishermen in the town. They were out before the sun came up.

He came to a stop and was out of the swing and down the hill in

The Move

a flash. He crossed the highway carefully and ran down to the boat docks. The tackle store and cafe were locked up. A sign on the door read, "Closed Temporarily—Under New Management." Jim had decided to take a week or two to get things in order before opening for business.

There was a small shed beside the tackle shop, right on the water near the docks. The shed, Peter learned, was used for working on the boats. The outboard motors, gas tanks, fishing nets, and life preservers were stored in the shed as well. It would be Peter's job to help his dad scrape and paint the bottoms of the boats. A block and tackle rig hung in the shed. It was used to raise the boats up out of the water for maintenance.

Peter walked slowly from boat to boat, taking everything in. He jumped into one now and then just to feel the water under his feet. He marveled at the gulls and the pelicans which were perched or soaring around. He had seen all this before on the yearly trips to the river, but this was his home now. He was in a daze at the thought of it when he heard his father call.

As Peter scrambled up the driveway to his new house, he could smell the delicious odor of bacon cooking. The sun was well up over the hills upriver now, and the warm sea air seemed to lift him up and carry him along. Before he knew it, he was at the kitchen door.

Peter burst into the kitchen and began to tell his family how beautiful their new surroundings were. He was so excited that his father finally had to tell him to calm down so that he could eat.

The entire day was like a dream. Peter saw that his father was as happy as he was as they unloaded the family belongings and brought them into the house. Bruce and June came to help with the unpacking and the arranging of the furniture. June helped Nancy in the kitchen; arranging, cleaning, and giving advice to the men as to where things should go. Jim and Bruce talked of what would have to be done to get the shop and the cafe ready for business. Anne played with her dolls in the front room. Fresh sandwiches and cookies were on the kitchen table whenever anyone was hungry.

When all was done, the Bobos stayed for a while. As they were about to go home, Bruce brought in something wrapped in newspaper. He crossed over to the fireplace and, removing the newspaper, placed the object on the mantel. It was a piece of rough pine wood beautifully carved with the words *Home Sweet Home*.

That night, in his own bed, in his new room, the bay shining in the moonlight outside his window, Peter dreamed of that carved piece of wood over the fireplace. He smiled in his sleep as he dreamed of his home sweet home.

5
New Country

In spite of the many vacation trips which the Miles family had made to the river, this was still new country to them. Peter became more and more aware of its newness as the days of early October passed.

Changing schools was an all new experience. The school stood atop a hill across the bay from home. From his desk by the window, Peter could see his house and all the activity in the bay. He could even see his father working around the new family business. It was all Peter could do to pay attention to the teacher.

Mrs. Pomroy was a very understanding, older lady. She knew that Peter was going through a time of many changes. She could see that he was trying to be a good student, and she was patient with him about gazing out the window. The kind lady knew that he would adjust as he became better acquainted with his new surroundings.

Most of the kids in his class were interested in Peter's former home in the big city. They asked many questions. "What about the amusement parks?" "How could you decide which movie to see first?"

Peter was a little shy at first, but he soon began to enjoy amazing his new school chums with stories about "the big city," as they called it. Still, he was far more interested in the place where they lived—where he lived now too.

The girls asked most of the questions. That made some of the boys a little jealous, and they sometimes teased Peter about being a "city slicker." That didn't bother Peter much. He did kind of wish, however, that he could brag about the big fish that his dad had caught or the deer which he had helped to track and shoot, the way the other boys did.

After school, Peter heard several of the boys making plans for their free time after they finished their chores at home. A couple of guys were going to shoot their pellet guns in the woods. Some were going to the movie at the only theater in town. Some were coming back to school to play ball or something.

Nobody bothered to ask Peter to join him. That made Peter a little sad. He even felt lonesome for his old friends in the city at times during those first days at school. He was never sad for long though. He was too busy taking in the beauty of the new country after school let out.

The sea breeze, with its peculiar salty-fishy smell, made Peter feel lighthearted, as he walked home across the bridge at the mouth of the river. The pine trees and the low mountains that bordered the river as it snaked inland were his company on his walk. The seagulls and pelicans were fun to watch from the bridge. Peter was especially fascinated by the pelicans.

Always before, when he was there on vacation, Peter had watched the pelicans. Now he had all the time in the world to watch them. He did not feel the need to hurry and take everything in at once as before. He would not be leaving the river in a few days. He would be there for a long time.

While studying the birds, Peter decided that pelicans were about the most curious-looking creatures in the world. They seemed to be two birds in one. Up front were tremendous bills with their lunch sacks attached. Following along behind were the parts that fly and swim. By far the most amazing were those scoop-like bills.

At that time of year, there was much activity in the waters at the mouth of the river. Salmon were waiting and eating. When they had put on enough extra weight to sustain them on their journey, and when the water was deep and cold in the river, they would swim upriver to their spawning grounds. The steelhead trout lived in the river all year round. Many smaller varieties of fish also inhabited the

New Country

waters—food for the steelheads and salmon. The smaller fish were the pelicans' main diet also.

Peter stood on the bridge and set his books on the wall. There he would stay for as long as an hour at a time. The pelicans soared high over the water. Each stayed in its own area, flying in wide circles over that part of the bay.

Suddenly, one of the circling pelicans would fold its wings and dive with its neck outstretched. Peter could scarcely believe how fast the pelican dived—like an arrow. As it streaked downward, the pelican might slightly unfold one wing or the other to correct its flight toward the target.

With a splash and a flurry, the pelican would hit the water, soon to emerge with a fish tail sticking out of its huge bill and a wriggling bulge in the pouch below. One gulp and the fish was gone. The bird would ruffle its feathers with satisfaction and fly back into the air, flapping furiously, to repeat the spectacle. Peter was sure that the pelican was the greatest fisher on earth.

When Peter arrived home each day, Nancy had a snack of some kind waiting for him in the kitchen. Peter liked the kitchen in his new home. There was a lot of room in it. Nancy liked the many cabinets of dark wood and the long counter beside the sink.

A large window next to the back door looked out at the huge pine trees on the hill behind the house. A thick, delicious fragrance of pine mixed with salt air wafted through the open window. The sun's warm rays lighted the kitchen in the afternoon. The family ate most of their meals on a round oak table by the window (the dining room being reserved for meals with company).

Large, glass-enclosed cabinets displaying Nancy's good dishes stood against one wall. A sturdy, oak chopping block squatted in the middle of the floor. Peter especially liked the wood beams of the ceiling. They reminded him of a mountain cabin.

After his snack, Peter took his schoolbooks upstairs to his room and changed into his work clothes. Then he ran down the hill and across the highway to the new family business. There Peter found his dad hard at work, getting things ready to open the doors for business.

Peter helped take inventory of the fishing tackle and the boating equipment in the store. Then there were the boat shed and the docks. Peter learned how to hoist the rental boats out of the water in the shed. The block and tackle made it easy. He and his dad scraped the bottom of each boat to remove the barnacles and algae. They painted one boat each day and left it hanging overnight to dry. The outboard motors were also cleaned well. Jim showed Peter how to start them. Jim had to do a little maintenance work on a couple of the motors. Thanks to his mechanical ability, he soon had all of them in good working order.

Peter cleaned up the shed, neatly arranging the life preservers, oars, gas tanks, and fishing nets. The fishing poles and tackle for rent were repaired and made ready in the tackle shop.

In the evenings, Nancy would come down to the shop with Anne in her arms. Then everyone worked hard in the little cafe next to the tackle shop. There was a lot of cleaning to do. Nancy wanted the place spotless. Peter washed the big bay windows overlooking the docks. He didn't mind that because he could watch the commercial fishing boats come home to their docks across the bay while he worked.

Jim and Nancy decided that the cafe would only be open in the mornings for breakfast. That way, Nancy would have some time in the afternoons to do her housework and to relax a bit before preparing dinner for the family. Anne would have to be in her playpen in the cafe. It was set up in the corner near a window where she could look out at the water and the boats.

Nancy spent one evening making up a menu for the small cafe. In keeping with the name of the business, the menu was printed with these words at the top: *Best Breakfast for Miles.*

6
First Fish

A week had passed since the Miles family had moved into their new home. Peter was at home for the weekend. After breakfast, Jim said that everything was ready for the shop to be open for business Monday morning. With Peter's help, the work had gone quickly.

Jim smiled across the breakfast table at Peter and said, "Son, I am proud of you. You have been a big help to me this past week. When we start the business next week, you will probably be busy with the boat rentals and with helping me in the store. You won't have much time to yourself. How would you like to go fishing today in *Kitty Clyde's Sister*?"

"Boy! Would I!" Peter shouted with joy. He hadn't really minded the work he had done that week. It had been more like fun. He hadn't been able to go fishing though, and that was his favorite thing to do in all the world.

Nancy told Peter to get a sweater from his room. Lately, when the sea breezes came up, the air was turning a little colder in the afternoons. She packed some sandwiches and a couple of apples for their lunch. Jim got candy bars and soda pop from the tackle shop, as he was getting their fishing poles and some anchovies for bait.

Launching *Kitty Clyde's Sister* at the boat landing near the bridge only took a few minutes. Jim and Peter felt proud each time they went out in their beautiful boat. Today was no exception. Peter felt kind of special when he got to go fishing with his dad. Often on their vacation trips, the entire family had rented a small boat like the ones at their docks and fished for salmon in the mouth of the river. This time it was just Peter and his dad in their own *Kitty Clyde's*

Sister. That was a great thrill. Peter would be happy whether they caught anything or not. Still, he could not help wishing that he could catch a big salmon to brag about to the boys at school.

Jim eased the boat into the bay and set a course along the rocks which formed the jetty on one side of the bay. In the years that he had been bringing his family to the river, Jim had learned from the local fisherman that most of the salmon in the bay stayed close to the jetty to feed before moving up the river. It was still early in the season, and most of the salmon would still be out in the ocean beyond the breakwater. Jim explained this to Peter and told him not to expect too much. "The smaller silver salmon come in first, and there are a few of them in the bay already," Jim said. "The larger Chinook salmon are the last to enter the bay, and it may be December before we will catch any of them.

As they cruised along the jetty, Jim and Peter let their lines out. Jim had hooked a single anchovy on the two hooks at the end of each line. He made it appear to the salmon as though the bait were swimming through the water. Peter could see his anchovy gliding through the water in a slow spiraling motion as he let his line out. "If there are any salmon out there, they cannot help but go for my bait," he thought.

Settling back in his seat against the cushion of the life preserver that he wore, Peter held his pole tip up. His gaze was fixed upon the point where his line disappeared into the water. He could imagine his bait, not too far behind that point, slowly spinning through the water. Jim let his own line out over the side as he steered *Kitty Clyde's Sister* along the jetty.

They sat for quite a while, as the boat made several large loops around the bay, coming close to the jetty each time. Jim checked the bait after each pass to make sure that it still looked fresh and had a good motion in the water. They ate their lunch as they went.

At least an hour and a half passed without a single strike. Several other boats were out on the water. Jim could see that they too were doing little good.

First Fish

Jim was reminding Peter that the real fishing would not start until late November and telling him not to be discouraged, when he saw his son's pole tip take a sharp dip. Peter was so excited that he forgot what to do. Jim quickly reminded him to let out some line.

When a salmon strikes, it will often "mouth" the bait just to kill it or to look it over. By letting out some line, Peter could make his bait stay where it was when it was hit. That way the salmon would think that it was wounded or dead.

Jim slowed the motor as Peter sat breathlessly looking out to where his line entered the water. Then it happened!

All at once there was a strong pull on the line. The pole tip plunged toward the back of the boat, and the salmon broke the water about sixty feet behind the boat. Peter instinctively pulled back on his rod, setting the hook, as the salmon knifed out of the water in a cloud of spray against the blue sky. The fight was on!

Jim cut the motor so that the line could not be tangled in the propeller if the salmon got under the boat. "It's a big silver!" he yelled to Peter.

Peter was not a stranger to this kind of fishing. He had caught silver salmon on their vacation trips. Nevertheless, it had been a long time since he had caught a salmon.

The strain on his line was tremendous. His reel was set to let out line before it reached breaking point. Even with forty-pound test line, this salmon was pulling out line so fast that the reel was singing, "zzzzzzz."

Line was going out so fast that Peter wondered if there were enough line on his reel to hold this fish. His arms were straining and goose pimples lined the back of his neck. Two more times the big fish jumped, still pulling out line.

"Attaboy, Son, just keep the tip up!" shouted Jim.

Finally the salmon stopped pulling, and the line stopped paying out. Peter began to reel in some line. He did not feel a thing. "It's gone!" he shouted. He reeled furiously, hoping the fish was still there, but fearing it wasn't.

"Reel!" coached his father. Jim had a hunch that this fish was still hooked.

Sure enough, suddenly there was a strong surge on the line, and Peter had all he could do to keep his rod tip up. The salmon had turned completely around and was diving under the boat. That was normal behavior for salmon, and Peter's father had suspected it. Peter's heart started pounding again. He was sure that it had stopped when he had thought the fish was gone.

For ten minutes Peter pulled and reeled trying to land the big fish. Jim talked encouragingly to his son. Peter's back began to ache. He could barely hold his pole up off the side of the boat. He knew that he must though so that the fish would tire from pulling against the flexible rod tip.

Finally, the big silver salmon glided into sight just beneath the surface, beside the boat. Jim swiftly swung into action and gaffed the fish securely. As he hoisted the salmon over the side of *Kitty Clyde's Sister,* Peter slumped back in his seat. He was exhausted. He was not too tired to hear the cheer that went up though. He looked up to see all the fishermen in the other boats around the small bay standing up and waving their arms. They had watched the battle from their boats and were applauding Peter's fishing skill for landing the big silver. Peter smiled and waved back, feeling proud.

That was the only fish caught that day by Peter and his dad. They continued to fish through the afternoon and into the evening. Toward sundown, the breeze stiffened a little, and Peter was glad to have his sweater along.

The sun was sinking low over the watery horizon when *Kitty Clyde's Sister* came to rest alongside the rental dock. This was the first time Jim had docked the prized boat beside the new family business. He and Peter felt warm with joy and pride as they stepped off their wonderful boat onto the docks of their glorious new place of business. "She looks natural, doesn't she?" Jim commented with pleasure.

"She sure does," Peter chirped.

First Fish

Nancy had spotted *Kitty Clyde's Sister* slipping into the docks. She and Anne were coming down the hill.

Peter saw his mother and yelled out, "I caught one!"

"Hurray!" she responded.

With that, Jim held the big silver salmon up with the gaff hook. It was all that he could do to hold the fish up high enough for Nancy to see. It was a very heavy fish.

When Nancy arrived on the dock, she gave Peter a big hug and a kiss. "That's a beautiful fish," she said. "It will be good eating." She looked at the fish for a moment and turned to Jim. "Let's have it smoked," she suggested.

Jim agreed wholeheartedly. The Miles family liked to eat salmon, and Nancy was great at cooking up tasty meals with it. More than anything else, however, they liked smoked salmon.

Everyone piled into the pickup truck, and Jim put the salmon in the back on a wet gunnysack. The cannery was just down the highway about a quarter of a mile. The Miles family knew of the cannery from previous visits to the river. The cannery would trade canned salmon for fresh-caught salmon. They could get either smoked or regular, or a little of each. On each can there was a label. The label read: "Salmon, caught by _____," with a place for the fisherman's name.

The man at the cannery was a big, burly man. He took Peter's fish and weighed it on the scales out front. When the needle came to rest at twenty-nine pounds, Peter was very proud.

"Too bad," said the cannery man. Peter stopped smiling and looked at the man with surprise.

Seeing Peter's shocked look, the big man kind of laughed and explained, "Don't get me wrong, Son. It's a good fish. Say, you folks must be new around here, huh?"

"Yes, we just took over Dutchman's place," Jim answered.

"Oh, you're the Miles family from the big city! My name's Jack Johnson. I own the cannery. See?" and he pointed at the sign over the door of the cannery which read, "J.J.'s Cannery."

At that, all of the Miles family were introduced. Everyone but Anne said hello. She only giggled.

"What did you mean when you said 'too bad,' Mr. Johnson?" inquired Jim.

Then it was that Jack Johnson, or J.J., showed Peter and his family the "Big Fish" sign. Over by the scales, in front of the cannery, was a large hook hanging from a metal bar. A sign over it read, "Big Fish." "Whenever someone comes in with a salmon of thirty pounds or more, we take his picture with his fish on this hook," explained J.J. "Then we put the fisherman's name, the weight of the fish, and the date it was caught under it."

J.J. then took the family inside to show them the big board with all the pictures on it. Peter spotted pictures of several boys in his school standing beside fish ranging anywhere from thirty to forty-nine pounds. He could not help feeling disappointed that his fish weighed only twenty-nine pounds. As hard as it had been to land though, he couldn't imagine pulling in a bigger one.

"Then there are the clippings," said J.J., pointing to the glass counter near the cash register.

Several newspaper clippings were taped to the inside of the glass, where everyone could see them. Each clipping had a picture of a big fish and the person who caught it. There were several fifty and fifty-one pound fish, and there was even a fifty-eight pound salmon. The dates on the articles went all the way back to 1947.

"That was the year I opened for business. And those are the biggest salmon caught in these parts," said J.J. "There are bigger fish. Some of the Chinook, or king salmon, they catch up in Canada run sixty to sixty-five pounds. They don't come this far south though. Water's too warm."

Peter looked at the clippings closely, but he didn't see anyone from his school in those pictures. Some of the fish looked to be as big as Peter. Why, he only weighed 125 pounds himself. Nevertheless, Peter still found himself dreaming of his picture being on

First Fish

display there. Then he thought, "It would be enough just to have a picture taken with a fish on the 'Big Fish' hook out front." That was what he thought about all evening at home. In fact, he even dreamed of being in a picture with a 'Big Fish' in front of the cannery.

7
The Outsider

Before he knew it, Monday morning came, and Peter had to go back to school. This would be his second week at the school across the bay. Peter had a new feeling on his way over the bridge this morning. The weekend had been wonderful—especially his fishing trip with his dad on Saturday. This morning, however, he was not very happy about returning to school. He liked his new teacher, and the schoolwork was not hard. But the behavior of the other boys in his class made him unhappy. They were not friendly.

As is the case with most school classrooms, Peter's class had its inner circle of boys. The other boys seemed to follow these three. They were Johnny Mark, Doug Farrell, and Paul Bass.

Johnny was the most popular of the three. He was tall with blond hair and freckles.

For some reason unknown to Peter, Johnny had been extremely quiet around him from the start. Sometimes in class, Peter would glance over to the far row of desks where Johnny sat and catch him staring back with a frown. That made Peter uneasy. Although he tried to smile and be friendly, Johnny would not smile back.

At lunchtime things were worse. Johnny and the other boys sat at one end of the tables and goofed around, laughing and joking. Peter sat nearby. He would laugh with them or say something funny to the others. Then Johnny would say something like, "Let's play ball and leave this city slicker to eat his lunch."

Such remarks hurt Peter, but he did not say anything back. He couldn't say that he wasn't a city slicker because he was. Peter's

The Outsider

father had always taught him not to fight unless he had to defend himself or someone else. Still, there were times when he wanted to sock Johnny Mark in the stomach.

This Monday was no different. Rather than be hurt again, Peter sat far away from the other boys and gazed at the sea while he ate his lunch. No one came over to speak to him. Mrs. Pomroy finally stopped to say something to him on her way to the office. "Why aren't you playing with the other boys, Peter?" she asked.

Peter hesitated and then he said, "I just like to watch the ocean, Mrs. Pomroy." That was not true, but Peter did not want to sound like a crybaby.

"OK, Peter," was her reply, and she patted him on the shoulder as she went on her way. Mrs. Pomroy knew what the problem was, but she thought that it was best for the students to work these things out for themselves. "If things get worse, I will have a talk with Johnny Mark," she reasoned.

As Peter gazed at the ocean, he found himself thinking that the vast water had a different personality now. Always before, he had found warmth and comfort in the huge, sighing body of water. Now it appeared wide and empty and lonely. It reminded him of his own loneliness, and he wished that he were back at his old school with all his old friends.

Johnny Mark was one of the boys Peter had seen pictured by a "Big Fish" at the cannery. What Peter did not know was that Johnny was not a very happy boy.

At home Johnny had two older brothers and his father and mother. Johnny's father was a big man. He worked at one of the local sawmills, and he was generally known as a mean person. He had been in a logging accident a few years back, and had lost one of his arms. Mr. Mark was quite bitter about his misfortune, and he had taken to drinking heavily over the last few years.

At home Mr. Mark was also mean. Johnny had been in the woodshed with him for a whipping many times. Sometimes he got whipped for things that his older brothers had done wrong. Even his older brothers were mean because they were not happy in their father's home.

Bob and Bill Mark, being twins, looked to each other for the good times and the happiness that were lacking in their home. Unfortunately for Johnny, their happiness often seemed to involve mischief which was designed to leave their younger brother all the blame.

Johnny was only happy at school, where he was able to be the leader among the boys in his class. They all followed him because he was the biggest boy in the class, and he was very good at sports. He could be funny at times too. Johnny tried hard to make everyone like him at school because he was so lonely at home. This new boy, Peter, with all his stories of the big city and the fun things which he and his family had done there, was a threat to Johnny's popularity at school, or so he thought. He was afraid that Peter would steal the attention of his friends which he needed so desperately. Peter was not aware of all this. Indeed, all he could see was that Johnny Mark was very unfriendly and mean.

As he walked home from school that afternoon, Peter did not stop to watch the pelicans. He was too miserable. When he got home, his mother could see that he was unhappy. He didn't even want any freshly baked cookies for a snack.

When Nancy asked her son what was bothering him, Peter answered, "Oh, nothing." He did not know how to tell his mother that he just didn't fit in at school. He was even beginning to think that it was partly his fault for not being more friendly toward Johnny Mark and for thinking about punching him in the stomach. He changed the subject by asking his mother how she did at the cafe that first morning.

"It was kind of slow because we had just opened for business," Nancy answered, "but we did have three customers. They liked the food. One of them lives around here. He said that he would tell his friends about my good breakfast." There were only six tables in the

The Outsider

cafe. They were lined up along the windows, looking out on the bay. The small counter could seat six more. It was just right for Nancy. She could do the cooking, the serving, and the dishes for one morning without much effort. The customers exited the cafe by way of the tackle shop. On the way out, they paid for their meals at the counter in the tackle shop where Jim was. Jim and Nancy decided that if business picked up much in the cafe, Nancy would hire someone to help out.

Peter did not stay sad after school. He changed into his work clothes. Then he was off to the tackle shop to help his dad and to see how the new business was doing. This was the first day that the doors were open for business, and Peter found his father quite busy. Jim had already rented three boats for all day, and he had three more fishing parties in the shop wanting to rent fishing tackle and boats with motors for the evening fishing.

Peter helped out by getting life jackets and fishing nets from the boat shed. He put them in the three boats that would be going out. Then he checked to make sure there was plenty of gas in the gas tanks and started the motors. He felt good as he helped the customers get their fishing gear into their boats. Then he cast off the lines from the dock, wishing each party good fishing. He even showed one family, who had never been salmon fishing before, how to bait their hooks with the anchovies so the bait would appear to be swimming through the water. That made Peter feel less like a city slicker than he did when Johnny Mark and the others called him one.

By the time all the boats had come in and the gear was put away, Peter had forgotten all about how unhappy he had been earlier. Three salmon were caught that day by the boat renters. Peter offered to clean them for twenty-five cents apiece, and all three of the successful fishermen were glad to pay him for the service. Peter's dad had suggested the idea to him. He was excited when he saw how easy it was to make seventy-five cents in one day. He could imagine how well he would do when the fishing improved.

So it went for the next couple of weeks. School was not so bad because Peter could look forward to his job at the shop in the afternoons. There was only the lunch period to get through anyway. The rest of the time Mrs. Pomroy kept everyong busy with spelling, reading, math, geography, history, and art.

When Peter had been in school three weeks, he made a wonderful new friend.

Bruce and June Bobo came for dinner Friday evening that week. Bruce went down to the shop where Jim and Peter were still working. He helped them put away all the gear and close up shop. Then they all went up to the house for dinner.

Bruce had brought two whole chickens which his friends at the farmhouse restaurant upriver had sent with him for "the new folks from the big city." Nancy and June fried them for dinner. After a delicious meal in the dining room, everyone moved to the spacious living room. Jim and Bruce built a fire in the fireplace with Peter's help. The nights were beginning to get quite cold. A fire made the living room warm and cozy. Peter felt like a real country boy, getting the wood from the woodpile outside. In the house in the city, there had been no fireplace. When the weather was cold, they had simply turned on the gas heater.

The living room ceiling, like the ceiling in the kitchen, was supported by rough wood beams. The walls were paneled with dark wood. The fireplace was of large river rocks from upriver. It was nearly ten feet wide and as tall as Peter. Truly grand fires could be built in its wide mouth. The chairs and the couch were made of oak with thick, firm cushions—much like those in the Bobo's lodge.

That Friday evening, as everyone sat comfortably before the fireplace, Bruce asked Peter if he would like to go up the river on his mail boat the next day. Peter was crazy about the idea, but he did not want to leave his father to mind the shop by himself. Nancy solved the problem. She said that she could help out in the store and care for Anne at the same time. Jim had sensed Peter's recent unhappiness at school. He thought that this trip would be good for his son. He could imagine how hard it was for Peter to adjust to his new

The Outsider

surroundings. To Peter's delight, he was free to go.

He was up and fed and out of the house Saturday morning before the sun came out from behind the hills upriver. He went down to the mailboat landing filled with youthful exuberance. He met Bruce there. Bruce introduced Peter to the other mail boat pilots who were in the small office drinking coffee by the wood-burning stove. Peter was wearing a sweatshirt and his jacket, but the warmth of the stove was welcome. November had arrived and the weather was definitely getting colder. He had to sleep under three blankets at night to keep warm.

Bruce made some instant cocoa for Peter. When they had finished their hot beverages and talked and laughed a while, the river pilots each went down to the dock to check the boats.

Peter accompanied Bruce and helped put cushions on the bench seats for the tourists to sit on. Then Bruce showed his helper the jet engine in the rear of the boat. Peter didn't know much about jet engines, but this one sure looked big to him. It was clean and new looking.

Each pilot was responsible for his own boat, and Peter could see that Bruce cared very well for his. When Bruce started the jet engine, Peter's eyes got big. Boy, it was loud with the engine cover off! With the cover in place, it quieted down a bit. Peter could tell that it was a powerful engine. Each boat had room for thirty people. It had to be a powerful boat to carry so many upstream against the mighty river.

Shortly after daylight, all the passengers came on board, and Peter helped Bruce shove off. He then climbed in and stood beside Bruce in the rear of the boat where the steering was. The tourists were seated in front of them, facing forward. Bruce got on the bullhorn to introduce himself and to welcome everyone aboard. Then he said, "And this is my first mate, Peter Miles. Peter's father is a good friend of mine. He just opened a little store with tackle and boats for rent. If anyone cares to go fishing while you're here at the river, I recommend his place."

Everyone turned around to listen to Bruce. When he finished, they all smiled and said hello!

Peter was a little embarrassed, but he managed to smile and wave back at all the folk.

Bruce was an excellent pilot, which was a good thing. There were several narrow, raging spots in the river where he had to use full power to keep from hitting big boulders in the water. When they came to smooth waters, Bruce let Peter take the wheel several times. Peter was thrilled, and he felt proud at such a privilege.

Bruce stopped along the way to watch fishermen who were catching fish. When a fish was landed, the passengers applauded and cheered the fisherman. Sometimes a fisherman would hold up his fish. Then the tourists in the boat would ooh, aah, and applaud some more.

Cabins lined the river on the hills above the flood line. Now and then small children would appear on the porch of one of the cabins to wave at the boat. The passengers waved back, to the delight of the children.

When they had been gone over an hour, the river began to wind through canyons bordered by high, craggy peaks. Huge pine trees grew right down to the river's edge. The air was heavy with pine scent. Here the only sound was that of the jet engine and the occasional conversation of the passengers.

Bruce picked up the bullhorn to announce that they were now in wilderness country and to be on the lookout for wildlife. He slowed the jet engine to a quiet throb. Soon a mother deer and her fawn were sighted on the riverbank. The deer stood still and stared at the tourists, who stared back and took pictures. Coming around a bend in the river, they surprised a black bear fishing in the river. And further up the river, a big moose with many-pointed antlers was seen. Squirrels and birds filled the trees all along the way.

When they reached the farmhouse, Peter helped Bruce tie up the boat at the dock. The passengers were helped ashore, and everyone was directed up the landing to the covered eating area near

The Outsider

the main house. Rows of picnic tables were set with plates and silverware. The tourists were seated and their food was served family style.

Bruce led Peter around behind the main building to a smaller building out back where all the cooking was done. There Peter met Aunt Molly, a round, jolly woman.

Bruce had told Peter about Aunt Molly on the way up the river. Everyone called her aunt because she treated complete strangers like close kin. She was the owner of the old farm. She lived there year-around with her brother, Sam. Her husband had died several years ago. Now Molly ran the old farm with the help of Sam and the hired hands.

Molly and Sam made Peter feel right at home with their warm welcome. Then Bruce led Peter into a room beside the kitchen where a big table was set for a meal. That was where the mail boat pilots ate. Soon all the pilots arrived and were seated around the table. That was when he came in. Peter noticed him right away, and he could not help staring.

"Peter, this is Chautauqua," Bruce said, introducing the man who had just sat down at one end of the table. "Chautauqua is a hired hand here at the farm. His people once owned all the country around here."

The man named Chautauqua reached across the table with a large, weathered hand, smiled warmly, and said, "Hello," as he shook Peter's hand.

Peter said, "Hello," and he could not help smiling back at the man.

Throughout the meal Peter listened to the chatter of the riverboat men and especially to what Chautauqua said. Chautauqua didn't say much, but when he spoke, he sounded both wise and friendly. He was a big man and looked very strong. His voice was even strong and deep; yet, at the same time, it was warm. Peter could not stop looking at his face. It was weathered and tan like those of the boatmen—yet it was different. He had high, sharp cheekbones and a square, strong chin. His eyes were jet black and set deep behind his cheekbones. There were no whiskers on his face, as there were on the other men. His hair was almost black, and he wore it long, past his shoulders. Peter guessed from his name and his appearance, and from what Bruce had said about his people owning the land, that Chautauqua was an Indian.

After the meal of fried chicken and other farm-fresh dishes, Bruce and Peter walked over to the barn behind the farmhouse. Several horses were in a corral built onto the barn. A smaller pen nearby held a large sow and her piglets. There were chickens running loose everywhere Peter looked.

As Peter was taking all this in, a voice spoke to him from behind. He was startled because he had not heard Chautauqua approaching.

"So you are a young riverboat pilot today," he said.

When he saw that he had startled Peter, Chautauqua laughed and said, "Forgive me. I am afraid that the Indian in me has caused you alarm. I did not mean to sneak up on you."

Peter laughed and said, "Oh, that's all right." Then, unable to stifle his curiosity any longer, he blurted, "Are you really an Indian?" Chautauqua was the first Indian whom Peter had ever come face to face with. He had only seen the ones in television Westerns and in movies.

Again Chautauqua laughed his deep, friendly laugh. "Yes, Peter, I am of the Chinook tribe. My people lived along the river before your people ever settled in these parts."

Peter loved to listen to Chautauqua speak. He thought that he could learn more from this wise man than he could ever learn in school. He didn't know why. It was just a feeling deep inside him. "Gee, I would sure like to know more about your people," he said.

"Perhaps that can be," replied Chautauqua. "Bruce has told me about your family and your recent move here from the city. You have not been here for long. You have not had time to find many friends. I would be happy to have you stay with us here at the ranch

The Outsider

one weekend if you could get your parents' permission. Then, perhaps we could learn to know each other and become friends."

Peter sensed that Chautauqua meant what he said. He wished that he could say how much it would mean to him to have such a friend in this new country. His only reply was, "I would like that. I'll ask my parents when I get home."

"That will be fine," Chautauqua said. "I am here every weekend unless I am hunting. Bruce can tell me of your coming."

So it was that Peter came upon his first offer of real friendship since his family had moved to the river. His heart was filled with delight all the way home. He was even more excited about the prospect of spending a weekend with Chautauqua than he was about steering the jet boat on the way downriver. Imagine having a real friend in this new country—and that friend a real Indian!

8
Chautauqua

Jim and Nancy were pleased to see their son so happy and excited when he returned from his river trip. When he told them of his new acquaintance and asked if he could stay overnight with Chautauqua the next weekend, they could not say no. Settling into a new place was not easy for Peter. He needed his parents' support in order to make the adjustment to his new surroundings. Jim and Nancy knew this, and they were glad to see their son make new friends. So it was all settled. Nancy would help out with the business the next weekend, and Peter would go with Bruce on Saturday to spend the night at the farmhouse up the river.

The week before his return upriver went slowly for Peter. His days at school were becoming unbearable. It was hard to concentrate on his school subjects in such an unfriendly atmosphere. Mrs. Pomroy had to speak to him twice during the week about not paying attention. Peter could not help it. He would look out the window, and his thoughts would turn to the coming weekend with Chautauqua.

Friday finally arrived. Peter hurried home after school to get everything ready for his trip. He did all of his homework for Monday. He helped his mother pack his clothes for the weekend. At last all was prepared.

That night Peter slept lightly. He dreamed of his coming adventure with Chautauqua. He even saw himself in Indian dress stalking a deer with bow and arrow. When he awoke in the morning, he raced downstairs. After a quick breakfast, which Nancy had to

Chautauqua

force him to eat, he said good-bye and raced down to the mail boat landing.

Bruce had told Chautauqua of Peter's plans to come up for the weekend on one of the trips earlier in the week. He could see that Peter was excited about the trip. Jim Miles had confided in Bruce about Peter's apparent lack of enthusiasm for school. Jim suspected that his son was having a hard time fitting in with his new schoolmates.

Bruce was happy to see that Peter was looking forward to the weekend with Chautauqua. He had known Chautauqua for several years and knew him to be wise beyond his years. Perhaps this friendship between Peter and the Indian would be just what the boy needed to begin to feel at home in his new surroundings.

When they arrived at the old farmhouse upriver, Chautauqua was waiting at the dock. "Hello, Peter," he said, as he helped with the docking. "I am pleased that you could come."

"Me too," was Peter's reply. He felt good to be welcomed by the Indian in his warm and friendly manner.

The conversation around the river pilots' dinner table was lively that afternoon. There was much talk about the weather. Several references were made to the approach of the "chinook wind." That made Peter curious. He knew that the king salmon was also referred to as the Chinook salmon, but he had never heard of a chinook wind.

After the meal, as he was putting his things away in the small room built onto the side of the barn where Chautauqua slept, Peter asked the Indian, "What is the chinook wind?"

Chautauqua explained, "The chinook wind is a warm southwest wind which comes in winter and suddenly melts the snow. You see, Peter, Chinook is a name which is used often in this country. It is the name of my tribe. There are few of us now, but once we were the greatest tribe in this country. When the white man came, we traded with him and taught him of our land. That is why we now have the Chinook salmon and the chinook wind."

Peter was fascinated by this bit of information, and he had many other questions for the big man who knew so much about this country. Right then it was time to bid farewell to Bruce and his boatful of tourists. There would be plenty of time for questions later.

When the mail boats had departed on their return trip, Peter suddenly realized that he was all alone with Chautauqua and Aunt Molly and the others at the farm. They were all at home here. He was a newcomer, a stranger. He wanted very much for them to like him. He wanted to fit in. He couldn't help thinking of his experience with the boys at school. He even feared that there might be something wrong with him and that Chautauqua might not really like him either. He vowed to himself to be a good guest and not to be any trouble.

He got his first chance to help out when they got back to the farmhouse from the docks. The tourists always left quite a mess and a lot of dirty dishes behind them. It was Chautauqua's job to help clean up along with Aunt Molly, Sam, and the others. Without being asked, Peter pitched in and began to help clearing the tables and carrying the dirty dishes to the kitchen to be washed.

Aunt Molly saw him and said, "Peter, you are our guest. You needn't help."

Peter replied, "I want to."

Chautauqua smiled.

Seeing Chautauqua's smiling approval, Peter felt good as he marched off with a stack of dishes.

There had been a large crowd on the boats that day, and the cleanup was a big job. Peter worked hard and steadily. He didn't quit until the last dish was washed, wiped, and put away.

Chautauqua was impressed by his young guest's helpfulness. When the cleanup job was completed, he said, "You are a fine worker, Peter, and you deserve a rest after all that hard work. Would you like to take a ride up the river with me now?"

"A ride?" Peter said, puzzled.

"Yes, on horseback," Chautauqua replied.

Chautauqua

"Wow, sure I would!" Peter exclaimed.

Chautauqua made arrangements with the other hands to take care of his remaining chores for the afternoon. Then he saddled a brown mare and led her out of the corral. He mounted and gave Peter a lift up behind him. They rode out along the trail that ran along the river. Peter felt like a real country boy seated behind the big Indian on the spirited horse.

The river was beautiful, and the country was rugged. Across the river, rocky cliffs rose up to sharp peaks topped with snow. The craggy mountainside was a fitting background for the rock-strewn rapids that broke up the river's course all along the way. On the near side, large pine trees forested uneven terrain. Willows grew along the riverbank. Peter saw several squirrels and many birds as they rode.

After they had ridden a short while, Chautauqua reined in the mare, and the two of them dismounted. "Let's walk from here and see what we can see," he said. He tied the reins to a low branch of a pine tree near some grass to let the horse graze. As they walked, Chautauqua showed Peter how to choose his steps in order to avoid stepping on twigs and dry leaves. That way no noise would give away their presence to any wildlife in the area. They walked upriver into the wind. Chautauqua explained that this would prevent their scent from going before them to signal their approach.

Peter tried very hard to walk quietly, and he did not step on any twigs or dry leaves. Still, he could not be as quiet as Chautauqua. His Indian friend wore soft leather moccasins. Even though he was twice as big as Peter, his footsteps were noiseless. Peter's hard-soled cowboy boots crunched and thudded on the hard ground.

Nevertheless, the two wildlife stalkers did come upon some deer drinking from the river in the fading evening sunlight. Three does—each with a fawn—gracefully quenched their thirst at the river's edge. A large buck with many points to his antlers stood still, sniffing the air and turning his head from side to side, alert to any possible danger.

As they watched the deer from behind a fallen tree, Peter imagined that he and Chautauqua were two Indian hunters out to supply their camp with meat. What a thrill it was to be out here in the woods with his Indian companion, stalking deer, their horse tethered down the trail. Peter wished the boys at school could see him. He knew that they wouldn't believe him if he told them about this adventure. They would think that he was just a city slicker making up a story.

When they returned to the farmhouse that evening, Peter helped Chautauqua rub down the mare and put her in the barn. Her name was Little Mother. Peter asked Chautauqua how she got her name. Chautauqua explained that he was responsible for the care and feeding of the horses. "It was winter time two years ago and Little Mother was in foal. When her time came, it was very hard. She nearly died. Her foal was very large, and she was almost too small. That is why, when her colt was born and she had recovered, I changed her name to Little Mother. She was called Brownie before that.

"You see, Peter, with my people it is not uncommon to change one's name. My parents changed my name when I was a boy about your age. They had taken me with them on a journey by train, to the East to see the white man's council house. That is what they called the White House. That was the only trip my parents ever took on a train.

"While we were in the East, we attended a traveling tent show. It was sort of a combination revival and minstrel show. My parents did not speak English well, and it thrilled them that I was able to understand what the preacher was saying in the revival meeting. The people in those parts called such tent shows chautauquas.

"From that time on my name was Chautauqua. When a Chinook has an experience which is unusual and important in his life, it is our way to give him a new name which speaks of this event."

Chautauqua led Peter out of the barn and pointed to a big

Chautauqua

stallion in the corral. "That is Little Mother's son," he said.

Peter saw that the stallion was much larger than Little Mother. "What is his name?" he asked.

"Big Trouble," was Chautauqua's reply.

Peter could not help laughing, and Chautauqua laughed with him.

That evening Peter went with Chautauqua up to the farmhouse. The hired hands were gathered in the big front room, along with Aunt Molly and Sam. They sat before a crackling fire in the large stone fireplace, laughing and joking about the tourists of the day.

"Did you see how much they ate today?" Aunt Molly asked everyone.

They laughed and said that it was quite amazing. It made them feel good that each group of tourists enjoyed themselves so much.

Often someone from one of the mail boat groups would tell Aunt Molly or Sam or one of the hands that a friend had recommended that they come up the river to eat at the old farmhouse. And after eating such a wonderful meal, they were glad that they had come. Peter could remember the thrill of his first meal at the farmhouse. He had eaten until he thought that he might burst. Peter's mother was a good cook, but that had to have been the best food he had ever eaten.

After a while the conversation got around to the chinook wind again. Peter just had to ask why it was so important.

Chautauqua explained, "The chinook wind melts the early snows high in the mountains, causing the river to swell. Then the salmon swim up the river to spawn. Many of the local residents lay in a year's supply of salmon during this first big run of salmon. The commercial fishermen and the cannery are also very busy at this time. Everyone looks to see who catches the biggest fish of the season as well. It is a local tradition which carries much honor for the fisherman whose skill lands the biggest salmon."

Peter was keenly interested in this talk. "How do you know that it is a chinook wind?" he inquired.

"You will feel it," Chautauqua replied. "It is a very warm wind. Then the river swells, and within a day or two the salmon start up the river."

Peter found himself thinking about the chinook wind for the rest of the evening. Later, when he and Chautauqua retired to the bunkhouse, having said good-night to Aunt Molly and the others, Peter told Chautauqua, "I would like to catch the biggest salmon."

Chautauqua replied, "If the Great Spirit wills it and gives you the strength, you will."

Peter wondered what Chautauqua meant, but he did not want to sound foolish.

Chautauqua explained that they would be up early the next morning and that Peter should get some rest.

Peter covered up in his bunk and, saying good night to Chautauqua, was soon sound asleep.

Chautauqua had something that he wanted to do. He put some more wood in the stove to keep the bunkhouse warm, as he sat down at the table nearby and began to work.

When the warm sunlight broke through the chill mountain air that Sunday morning, Peter awoke in his bunk and sat up to peer through sleepy eyes at his unfamiliar surroundings. There, at the foot of his bed, was a pair of moccasins. Peter wondered whose they were and why they were there.

"Do you like them?" asked Chautauqua in his warm, husky voice. He stood near the wood-burning stove, already fully dressed and holding a steaming cup of coffee.

"Are they for me?" asked Peter in wonder.

"If they fit and you want them," was the big Indian's reply.

"Wow!" Peter exclaimed, throwing back the blankets and reaching for the moccasins. He slipped them on. They fit snugly, but well. "I sure do want them, but I have nothing to give in return."

"Your friendship will be payment enough, Peter," Chautauqua said. "The moccasins are a gift. Between friends the giver is rewarded in the giving."

"I am proud to be your friend, Chautauqua," Peter said feelingly.

"And I yours," was the reply.

"You are my first real friend since I left the city," Peter confided as he sat facing Chautauqua on the edge of the bunk.

Chautauqua smiled and said, "Real friendship grows out of common experience, Peter. You and I are alike. I am a stranger to this white man's world by birth. You are a stranger to this river country. We can fill each other's need for friendship because of this common bond." Peter smiled and nodded his understanding.

By now Aunt Molly was busy making breakfast in the kitchen of the farmhouse. The smell of frying bacon seeped into the bunkhouse.

Chautauqua told Peter to wash up and they would go have breakfast.

Peter, who was always hungry, quickly obeyed. How wonderful his new moccasins felt as he crossed the short distance to the main house. He could walk so softly that he could scarcely hear his own footsteps. Chautauqua saw the pleasure in Peter's face. He smiled.

Breakfast was delicious: fresh eggs, bacon, and biscuits with churned butter and wild blackberry preserves. Peter had hot chocolate and the others drank coffee. Everyone was cheerful and happy as they talked of the preparations for the day's tourists.

Aunt Molly explained to Peter that they worked seven days a week during the tourist season. When the snows came in late December and January, the farmhouse restaurant closed down because there were no tourists. "We cannot get out to church on Sunday because we have to work, Peter. Instead, we read the Bible for a time after breakfast all together here at the table. Do you go to church, Peter?"

Peter hesitated, "We used to go every week in the city," he replied, "but Dad has been pretty busy with the new business since we got here." Peter didn't mind going to church. On the other hand, he didn't really enjoy going. The singing was all right, but he often fell asleep during the preaching.

"Aunt Molly," Chautauqua said, "I would like to take my young brother to my church this morning."

Aunt Molly smiled her approval.

Peter blushed with pride at the big Indian calling him his brother. He wanted very much to go with Chautauqua, although he had no idea where his church was or what it would be like.

"Does that meet with your approval, Peter?" asked Aunt Molly, noting his obvious joy.

"Sure," Peter answered.

As they left the farmhouse, Chautauqua told Peter that it was not far to his place of worship, and they could walk. Peter was glad for the chance to try out his new moccasins some more. They started up the trail along the river and soon reached the spot where they had tethered Little Mother the evening before. It was still early morning. The air was chilly and the ground was hard. Peter wore his warm jacket. Chautauqua wore a long buckskin shirt over his plaid cowboy shirt.

"Walk softly, Little Brother," he told Peter, "the wild things may be near the river for their morning drink."

Peter did as he was told. Indeed, he had been walking softly ever since they had left the kitchen. It was easy with the new moccasins.

The breeze was at their faces, and the trees were alive with the sounds of birds and squirrels. A woodpecker noisily hammered on a tall pine tree. As the two rounded a bend in the trail, Chautauqua quickly stepped behind a low bush, pulling Peter with him.

There, in the shallows of a wide pool, was a huge black bear with her two yearling cubs nearby. She was teaching them to fish. She rose up on her hind legs and stood perfectly still, peering into the clear water. The two young bears were on the bank behind her. Suddenly, with a swift slap of her big paw, the mother bear swatted a large steelhead right out of the water and tossed it onto the shore in front of the youngsters.

Peter stared breathlessly as the cubs pounced on their breakfast. Chautauqua looked at Peter and smiled. The two friends remained crouched behind the bush watching while the mother bear repeated her performance two more times. Then the three bears ambled off leaving only the heads of the fish on the riverbank.

Chautauqua led Peter quietly and cautiously past the scene of the black bears' breakfast and on up the trail. They came upon a few deer in the same spot where they had seen the others the evening before. When the deer had quenched their thirst and moved away, Chautauqua told Peter, "This is where we must cross the river." A fallen log lay across the drinking pool where the deer had been. Peter followed Chautauqua, placing each foot where he did and holding on to broken limb stubs.

Now they were on the steep, mountainous side of the river. A narrow trail could be seen on the mountainside, running along the river and up the mountain. They walked carefully. Chautauqua took Peter's hand and walked ahead of him, kicking loose rocks off the trail. The rocks bounced down the mountainside to splash in the river. In a short time, the two were high above the river. They came to the top of a low ridge and crossed over it. Far below a stream tumbled down a narrow canyon branching off from the river canyon. Looking up this canyon, Peter could see a white mist rising from behind a stand of huge pine trees. A low roar echoed down the canyon from the source of the mist.

"There is my church," Chautauqua said.

Peter looked questioningly at his big friend, but Chautauqua offered no further explanation. He just motioned for Peter to follow and started off along the ridge trail toward the trees beneath the white mist.

As they approached the place where the mist rose, the dull roar got louder and clearer. Now Peter could make out the sound of water crashing and splashing on water and rocks. He knew that this must be a waterfall, although the tall pine trees hid it from sight.

Chautauqua carefully led Peter down the ridge to the grove of trees surrounding the waterfall. The sound of the crashing water was quite loud now. Chautauqua said nothing, for he knew that it was hard to hear someone speak near the waterfall. Peter did not want to shout—especially in Chautauqua's church—so he, too, was silent. Thus cloaked in a kind of reverent silence, the two entered the cathedral of trees.

Chautauqua climbed up on a flat rock of great size near the base of the waterfall and gave Peter a hand up. There they watched the water come tumbling down.

When the water hit the jagged rocks at the end of its fall, it splashed and sprayed out. Some of the water fell into the deep pool in front of the fall, while much of it exploded into a fine mist which billowed up into the air. The mist was caught by air currents to rise swirling and turning to fully the height of the top of the waterfall. The trees around the pool were very old and had grown huge with plenty of water. Still, the mist carried over their topmost branches. There sunlight transformed the mist into a shimmering rainbow which covered the space between the waterfall and the majestic trees. Peter thought that it was like the beautifully colored ceilings of the old churches which he had seen in his schoolbooks. The bright, sparkling colors of the rainbow truly made this a beautiful church.

Chautauqua sat very still on the flat rock beside Peter. His legs were crossed and his back was straight. He stared straight ahead, looking up at times. Although his eyes were not closed, Peter was sure that he must be praying. Peter sat quietly. He did not grow tired of looking and listening in this beautiful place. He did not fall asleep in this church. He watched the water falling. He gazed reverently at the giant pine trees. Most of all, he beheld the swirling, misty rainbow above.

A new and wonderful feeling came over Peter in this place of unparalleled beauty. As warm shafts of sunlight penetrated the multicolored canopy, they seemed to carry the many colors with them. Peter marveled that he seemed to be bathing in a shower of bright warm colors. Never before had he been so completely surrounded by such magnificence. He felt small and insignificant in the light of this glorious scene. Yet, at the same time he was warmed and filled with joy as he beheld the power of the waterfall, the serenity of the tall pines, and the radiant beauty of the rainbow.

Peter was startled by Chautauqua's movement as the Indian rose gracefully from his cross-legged position. They had been seated on the flat rock for some time. Peter had been so taken in by the grandeur of the place that he had become oblivious to Chautauqua's still presence beside him. Now he rose to follow as his new friend led the way out of the grove and back along the ridge trail. Neither bothered to talk until they were some distance from the falls. When the roar had lessened, Chautauqua asked Peter over his shoulder as they walked, "Did you like my church?"

"Oh, yes! Very much!" was Peter's heartfelt reply.

"I am close to the Great Spirit here," said Chautauqua. "When I gaze up to the light of the rainbow, it takes me into itself and we seem to become one."

"Yeah," agreed Peter and he knew just what Chautauqua meant, though he marveled at how well he described the feeling.

"My people use the name Great Spirit for the one your people call God," Chautauqua continued. "All of my ancestors worshiped the Great Spirit, and my tribe always consulted him with prayers. Some of my people worshiped him differently than others.

"For instance, when the warm wind came and the first salmon came up the river, my people had a ceremony. The first salmon caught was carefully prepared by the women of the village. It was then brought before the fishermen who sat silently in a circle. Each man ate a morsel of this first fish, giving thanks to the Great Spirit for bringing the salmon to our waters again. In this circle, some were actually giving thanks to the fish they were eating. Others in the circle gave thanks to the Great Spirit for sending the fish, and they regarded the fish as a sign of his love for my people.

"I worship at the waterfall in this way, Peter. I see the Great Spirit in the mist of the waterfall. I see him in the wings of the hawk." By now the two had reached the crest of the ridge. Chautauqua pointed out a large hawk circling gracefully over the river below. "He made everything and everyone. He made everything to have a purpose."

As they stood at the top of the ridge looking out at the hawk soaring over the mighty river below, Peter listened attentively to all that Chautauqua said. Never before had God, or the Great Spirit as Chautauqua called him, been so real to Peter. He found himself wondering if God were even causing Johnny Mark to be mean the way he was.

The hike back to the farmhouse was quiet and uneventful. A peace came over the two friends as they made their way down the mountainside, across the river, and through the pine trees bordering the homeward trail. The thick fragrance of the trees and the many sounds of songbirds and squirrels carried them along, neither feeling the need to speak.

Chautauqua, who spoke few words as a rule, carefully choosing those that would best say what he meant, was silent now. He had said quite a lot back at the ridge, and it seemed to have exhausted his desire to talk for a while. Peter didn't mind. Indeed, his mind was occupied with many thoughts, and he was content just to walk with his friend. Truly, an unspoken bond had developed between these two. Friendship had quickly evolved into brotherhood.

Upon their return to the farmhouse, kindly Aunt Molly asked Peter if he had enjoyed going to church with Chautauqua. Being possessed of many years and the wisdom that accompanies them when one is attentive to life, Aunt Molly could sense that this had truly been a meaningful experience for Peter. She perceived this more in his thoughtful serenity than in his reply which was simply, "Yes, ma'am."

In contrast to the peaceful morning, that Sunday afternoon was full of activity. Preparations were made for the hungry horde of tourists soon to arrive for the meal at the end of their boat ride upriver. Peter worked hard to help get everything ready. He set tables and carried steaming plates of chicken and mashed potatoes out to them from the kitchen. The tourists arrived right on time.

After a quick meal with the hands and the river pilots, Peter and Chautauqua went to the bunkhouse to pack Peter's gear for the trip home. Peter packed his boots away, preferring to wear his moccasins for the boat ride.

As they were walking down to the docks with his things, Peter thanked Chautauqua for the weekend. "I had a wonderful time," he said.

"I too had a good time," said Chautauqua. "You must come and stay again, my brother."

"Thank you again for the moccasins," Peter added.

"I am glad that you like them," was Chautauqua's reply. "Your boots are good to wear in the city. I have wanted a pair myself. In the woods, moccasins are best."

Bruce and his passengers were ready to leave. Peter said goodbye to everyone from the farm, thanking them for his stay. Aunt Molly said that he was welcome anytime and hugged Peter in front of all the tourists, which made him blush. As they shoved off, Peter waved a last farewell to Chautauqua, who smiled and waved back.

All the way home, Peter smiled and told Bruce of the many wonderful events of the weekend. Bruce could see a change in Peter. The timid, apprehensive young boy who had ridden upriver with him the day before was now glowing with inner strength and confidence. Peter didn't know that it showed, but he did feel a new sense of well-being as a result of his weekend spent with Chautauqua.

9
Loneliness

Peter recounted the events of his weekend to his parents when he got home. The prospect of returning to school the next morning did not dim his excitement as he showed off the fine moccasins which his big Indian brother had made for him. Jim and Nancy could see that the trip had truly been a good experience for their son. They sensed a confidence in Peter, which he had not had before his weekend upriver. Their son was developing into quite a young man, and they were proud to see that he could stand by himself in new surroundings. From his account of the trip, Jim and Nancy knew that Peter was strong enough to make the adjustment to this new country.

Nancy told Peter he could invite Chautauqua down for dinner. Bruce could deliver the invitation when he returned upriver on one of his tourist runs. With that pleasant thought in mind, Peter went upstairs to bed. He placed his moccasins at the foot of his bed where he could gaze at them. Exhausted by his full weekend, he soon fell fast asleep.

The next morning Peter was faced with the reality of another week at school. Back in the city, Mondays had not caused any particular bad feelings. Peter had enjoyed getting back together with his friends to recount their weekend activities. His only reluctance had been upon those rare occasions when he had not completed all of his homework. This morning he did not have to worry about that. His lessons were all done. He did have another cause for reluctance.

Peter knew that to wear his new moccasins would give Johnny Mark and the other boys ammunition for their teasing remarks. He was disappointed at having to leave his prized possession at home,

Loneliness

but he did not want to make matters worse. Pulling on his cowboy boots, he trudged downstairs.

As Peter dutifully ate his breakfast, Nancy saw the look of unhappiness on his face. It hurt her to see her son so uneasy about his school days. She did not know how to help him though. Jim had advised her that this was something that Peter would have to work out for himself. Still, it was painful for Nancy to watch her son march off to school with such a long face. "I love you, Peter!" she called after him as he walked down the hill to the highway.

That day and all the days that week were as before for Peter. His schoolwork was not hard. He always had the right answers when Mrs. Pomroy called upon him in class. He spent his lunchtime sitting and eating alone while looking out to sea. The boys still excluded him from their ball games. Johnny Mark seemed to take special pleasure in teasing him now because he could see that it was getting to Peter. Peter did not want to talk with the girls in his class too much. He was afraid that would make him look like a sissy.

After school the usual chores at the family business and homework kept Peter busy. Even the boat docks were losing their charm. Peter had been helping out around the docks for more than a month now. The newness had worn off. Depression brought on by his school situation even made the work less interesting to Peter than it had been. The only fun part of his work was cleaning fish for the folk who rented the fishing boats. The fishing was getting better. There were plenty of silver salmon and steelheads to be cleaned. It was a good feeling to bring in his own money each day. Peter was saving all of it for something special.

The weekend was very busy. Peter would much rather have gone up to see Chautauqua again, but there was too much work for him to do. The business was doing well now as more tourists arrived at the river in anticipation of the big day when the chinook wind would come to signal the salmon run. It could happen any time now.

Jim Miles was pleased with his new business. He often told Peter how much he valued his efforts around the docks. Peter's cheerless expressions were not so easily cured however. There seemed to be no cheering him up. School was becoming a real burden. Jim decided to do something about it.

Monday afternoon Jim closed the rental office and tackle shop for lunch and drove the pickup over to the school. He parked a distance away so he would not cause Peter any embarrassment. He made his way to the school office. He introduced himself as Peter's father and asked to speak with Mrs. Pomroy.

Mrs. Pomroy got a message to come to the office for a consultation just as she let her class out for lunch. "I've been expecting a visit from you, Mr. Miles," she said upon being introduced in the office. "You have come to see what is bothering Peter, haven't you? Such a fine young man! I knew that his parents were people who care about him. He is truly undergoing a trying situation, and yet he never complains. And he is such a good student," the kindly teacher continued.

"What is the problem then?" asked Jim. He perceived that this woman was wise and that she was genuinely concerned about Peter.

"I'll show you," was the teacher's answer. Mrs. Pomroy led Jim out the side door of the office to a point down the corridor where they could see the students without being observed themselves. She said, "There is the problem."

Jim saw students all around the schoolyard. The girls were jumping rope and tossing a large ball. The boys had a rousing game of softball going. All alone with his back to them, sat Peter staring out to sea, his lunch box lying open before him. Jim's heart went out to his son. "But why isn't he playing ball? Peter is a good ball player."

"They won't let him," Mrs. Pomroy answered.

"Who won't let him?"

"Well, mainly that tall, blond boy with freckles. You see, Mr. Miles, Johnny Mark is quite a leader at school. He really is a good boy. He is not happy at home though. He does not have a caring father like Peter has. I believe that he regards your son as a challenge

Loneliness

to his popularity at school. His insecurity has caused him to be very unfriendly toward Peter. He has even turned the other boys against poor Peter. Your son is such a friendly young man that he does not seem to know how to deal with such unfriendliness. Rather than cause trouble, he just sits alone and avoids a confrontation with Johnny."

Now it was obvious to Jim why his son was so unhappy about school. He and Mrs. Pomroy returned to the office. Both agreed that something must be done. Time had not resolved the situation. Mrs. Pomroy promised to have a talk with Johnny Mark and a couple of the other boys with the hope that she could make them see the error of their ways. Jim thanked her kindly. He knew that he could trust this wise lady to keep his visit in confidence.

The next day Peter received a great shock. At lunch time, as he sat quietly eating his lunch, Doug Farrell and Paul Bass came over to him. Expecting the worst, Peter looked up at the two boys. Imagine his surprise when Doug said, "You wanna play ball?"

After a moment of disbelief, Peter said, "Sure!"

It was a wonderful feeling to join with the guys on the baseball field. Peter could catch and throw and hit well. He liked baseball. He had such a swell time that it didn't matter that Johnny Mark glared at him all through the lunch hour. The other boys didn't tease him once about being a city slicker, although they were not overly friendly. Peter couldn't understand what had brought on this sudden change. He didn't really care. He just had fun playing ball instead of sitting alone with his thoughts. Peter wasn't even bothered that no one congratulated him when he made a good catch or got a hit.

The day seemed to go by much more quickly since the lunch hour was not such a long, lonely time. Peter was in better spirits that evening as he helped around the docks. Jim noticed the change in his son's mood, and he decided that his talk with Mrs. Pomroy had been a good idea. This was a great relief to Jim because he had worried that he might have been wrong to interfere in the natural course of things. He had hoped that Peter would find his own way at school. It certainly wasn't the boy's fault that his peers were unwilling to accept him because of the jealous whims of the class leader. Indeed, Jim had begun to feel responsible for his son's unhappiness for having disrupted Peter's established friendships back in the city. Anyway, it was all over now.

The rest of the week and the next week passed. Peter did not loathe the time spent at school anymore. He joined in the baseball game each day when the weather permitted. Two days were spent in the classroom that second week. The wind blew fiercely, and Mrs. Pomroy said that it would be snowing upriver on those days. Peter spent lunch hours watching the violent crashing waves. The wind blew directly off the ocean at the schoolhouse. Great clouds of salt spray flew by as the wind-whipped waves broke in a foaming, seething soup all up and down the coast as far as Peter could see.

The other boys were accustomed to this kind of stormy weather. It held no special interest for them. They played checkers and horsed around in the classroom to pass the lunchtime. Peter did not feel altogether at ease around his boy classmates yet. Oh, it was all right playing baseball out on the playground with them. There one was accepted for his abilities. This kind of roughhousing and wrestling was more intimate however. Only good friends could enjoy such close contact fun.

Peter was not sure whether it was just his imagination, but he had the distinct impression that the fellows in his class still regarded him as sort of an outsider. He couldn't quite put his finger on it, but he thought that they acted much like he did around his cousin Clara.

Clara, Jim Miles's sister's daughter, was an only child. Peter couldn't stand Clara. He had told his mother that he didn't like to play with Clara when she came to visit. "Clara is spoiled," he said. "She has to have her way or she cries." Nancy had explained to Peter that Clara was family; and that, even though she was spoiled, he must play with her and treat her kindly. Peter tried to be nice to Clara, but it was all he could do to tolerate her. That was how the boys in his class seemed to be treating him—they just tolerated him.

Loneliness

Nevertheless, Peter was not one to complain. He didn't mind so much that no one made an effort to talk to him off the ball field. At least he was part of the team when the weather was good.

Then one Thursday, as they were playing baseball, something happened to change things. Peter was at bat. His side was losing by one run. Johnny Mark was pitching for the other team. Lunchtime was nearly over. Johnny pitched fast, and even Peter had a hard time getting a hit against him. Doug Farrell was on first base. Johnny threw a fastball. Peter swung.

Whack! Peter knew it was a good hit by the sound. He ran so fast around the bases that he almost overtook Doug as he rounded third base. The ball came in from the outfield just as Peter neared home plate, the winning run. Johnny Mark had come in to get the throw. He stepped right in front of the catcher to tag Peter out. The throw took a high bounce. Peter slid in under Johnny's glove as he caught the ball. He was safe. He had won the game for his team.

"You're out!" yelled Johnny.

"I was safe," Peter argued.

"What do you know, city slicker, the only reason you're even playing is because Mrs. Pomroy made us let you, anyway," Johnny taunted.

Peter couldn't believe his ears. So that was why they asked him to play ball—Mrs. Pomroy told them to. Peter didn't say anything. He just brushed himself off and walked slowly away. He didn't even want to hit Johnny. What good would it do? They were all part of it. He would have to beat up all of them. Besides, that was not his way. Peter liked people. He did not enjoy hurting people.

That afternoon Jim saw a new look on Peter's face. The boy seemed hopelessly cheerless. When he asked his son what was wrong, Peter said, "None of the guys at school like me," and his eyes filled up with tears.

Jim's heart sank.

"What happened?" he asked.

Peter told his father all that had happened. When he was

finished, he looked to his father for his reply. He had always received good advice from his dad. Maybe he could straighten things out this time. Peter was certainly at the end of his ability to cope with the situation. It was all he could do to keep from crying as he related to his father the way things were at school.

Jim put his arm around Peter's shoulders. Obviously his talk with Mrs. Pomroy had only served to make matters worse for his son. He felt hopeless. How could he tell Peter about his attempt to solve the problem? What could he say or do to help now? The only hope that he could offer was that this situation would pass.

"Maybe it's not as bad as you think, Son," Jim said. "Certainly all the boys aren't against you. I know that it's hard to find your place in a new school, but you are a bright and friendly boy. I am confident that things will work out. Give it more time. Just keep doing your best and keep doing what you think is right. I am proud to have you for my son, and I am sure that you will overcome the obstacles that you are encountering at school. Just remember that your mother and I love you and that we're on your side no matter what."

Peter was reassured by this vote of confidence. He had hoped that there might be an easier solution to his problem. Nevertheless, he knew that his father was right. He would just have to keep trying. He didn't want to be a cause for concern to his family. Peter was glad that his father's new business was doing so well. It was a nice change to be able to see more of his dad in their new home. Jim's former job in the city had required him to be gone all day during the week. Each member of his family had to adjust to this new environment. Thus, Peter vowed to himself to be strong. He would not let Johnny Mark or the others get him down.

The next day was Friday, the last day of November. Only two more weeks of school before Christmas vacation. That was an encouraging thought for Peter as he walked to school that morning. As he crossed the bridge over the bay, something else stirred his thinking. It was quite windy. Nancy had made him bundle up in his

Loneliness

warm jacket and gloves this morning as she had every morning lately. The cold days of fall were giving way to the colder days of winter. The wind had blown so cold in the morning lately that Peter had found it necessary to put up his fur-lined hood. His face had turned red from the cold on those mornings.

Now here he was crossing the bridge where he was completely exposed to the full force of the wind. White caps were rolling up the river before the steady blow; and yet Peter did not feel cold. In fact, he even unbuttoned his jacket to keep from getting too warm. "The chinook wind," he thought. "This must be the chinook wind."

When lunchtime finally arrived, the wind was blowing with great force. There was to be no ball playing that day. Peter spent the hour watching the wind on the water. He walked down the open corridor to the bathroom for a chance to feel the air temperature. It was even warmer then than it had been that morning. He was convinced. This had to be the chinook wind. It was just as Chautauqua had described it.

Peter avoided Johnny Mark. His words of the previous day still rang in Peter's ears. Peter also avoided the glances from the other boys in the class. Therefore, he didn't see the looks of sympathy that came his way from Doug Farrell, Paul Bass, and others. Peter couldn't know that several of the boys were feeling badly about the treatment which he had received at the hands of Johnny.

The boys had easily teased this newcomer at first. But now that it had gone so far, some of the boys were feeling remorse for their harsh treatment of Peter. Not one of the boys knew that others among them also felt that their teasing had grown into a cruel game. In reality, each them was secretly glad that he was not the object of all that teasing. Rather than admit their guilt and risk being ridiculed, they all kept their thoughts to themselves.

When school let out that afternoon, the air was full of excitement. As the students gathered their belongings and put on their coats for the trip home, there was much conversation about the weekend ahead. Peter was not the only one who recognized the chinook wind. All of the local boys and girls knew of the event which the warm wind heralded. As Peter was going out the door, he heard Johnny Mark loudly proclaim for all to hear, "I will catch the biggest fish this year!"

When Peter reached home, he hurried down to the docks. He rushed into the tackle shop. "Dad, it's the chinook wind!" he proclaimed.

"It sure is, Son," was Jim's reply.

"The salmon will run tomorrow. Can we go out?" Peter pleaded.

"Well, Son, you know that there will be many fishermen in need of boats tomorrow," his father responded. Peter's heart sank. "The way I've got it figured though, we can rent out most of the boats in the morning for the whole day. Then we will take *Kitty Clyde's Sister* out and try for a big one ourselves."

"Ya-hoo!" Peter yelled.

Once again Peter was filled with his youthful enthusiasm. As he worked around the docks that evening, getting everything in readiness for Saturday morning, he kept looking out at the mouth of the river where the sea rolled over the sandbar. It was low tide, and the ocean swells were large as they rolled over the submerged belt of sand. Peter squinted and looked hard as if he expected to see great salmon surging into the bay amidst the waves.

When all of the rental boats were prepared, Peter and his father stored their own fishing gear aboard *Kitty Clyde's Sister*. Jim gassed her up. Now everything was ready to go. When the time came, they could cast off and head straight for the jetty.

As the boy and his father walked up the hill that evening with the wind at their backs, they were both filled with spirited anticipation of the coming adventure. They shared the same thought without speaking it. "As hard as it is to make the adjustments to this new life, it is worth the effort to feel so alive."

Later, as Peter lay in his bed unable to sleep, he was roused by a compelling urge. Slipping out from under the covers, he knelt

Loneliness

beside his bed. "Great Spirit," he began, "I know you won't mind that I call you 'Great Spirit' instead of 'God' because Chautauqua calls you that. Please help me understand my loneliness at school. Show me why Johnny Mark and the others are so unfriendly. And if you want to, make them like me. Thank you and good-night."

10
December King

The first day of December dawned with dazzling sunlight. The chinook wind had passed, leaving the blue sky without a trace of clouds. Seagulls screamed and pelicans circled and dived in a frenzied dance. The air was heavy with the smell of fish. The bay seemed to beckon to all fishermen who would listen: "Come! Fish! I am laden with salmon!"

Peter scrambled about on the docks that morning. A large crowd of fishermen gathered to rent boats. By ten o'clock, every boat was out. Jim Miles could scarcely believe the number of customers who were desperate for a boat. It was apparent that he would be better off to get away from the shop for the rest of the day. Already he had turned away two parties of fishermen. When he told them that there were no more boats, they were heartbroken.

Quickly, Jim put up the "closed" sign. He and Peter bid farewell to Nancy and Anne who had come down to see them off. Nancy hugged each of them and warned them not to come home without a big fish. With that the two eager anglers climbed aboard *Kitty Clyde's Sister*.

Peter's senses were keen as he untied the mooring ropes and pushed the beloved boat away from the dock. His heart began to pound when the powerful outboard motors started. He heard the gurgling, belching noises and smelled the rich, sweet smell of the fuel mixed with salt air.

Kitty Clyde's Sister plowed through the water, away from the docks and out into the bay. Small waves slapped against the hull. Peter smiled to himself as he remembered that the hull was painted blue to camouflage the boat against the sky.

Jim rang the brass bell as the two waved to Nancy and Anne who were back on the dock. Salt spray thrown up from the bow, as *Kitty Clyde's Sister* knifed through the water, clung to the brass railing to glisten in the sun like so many diamonds.

Peter stepped into the cabin to get the fishing gear. As he swayed about on his sea legs, gathering everything together, his nostrils filled with the thick fragrance of wood and varnish. A shiny brass porthole framed the watery scenery as it flew by. *Kitty Clyde's Sister* plunged and rocked as she passed through the wake of another boat. Peter remained on his feet. It was easy—he had his moccasins on.

Entranced by the delight of the moment, Peter relived his conversation with Chautauqua when he said, "You will catch the biggest fish if the Great Spirit wills it and gives you the strength." He felt stronger today than he had ever felt before. The excitement of the adventure made his heart pound, and his head was light. He could scarcely wait to get his bait in the water.

When Peter emerged from the cabin, his dad had cut one of the motors. Now he throttled down on the other.

"Steer a course for the jetty, Son, while I bait the hooks," he said.

Peter took hold of the ship's wheel and did as he was told. He was filled with satisfaction as he commanded this glorious vessel which he had helped to restore.

When they reached the jetty, Peter swung the boat around to parallel the rocky shoreline. By now his father had carefully baited both lines. Peter took up his position on the bench seat in the rear of the boat. The seat was fitted with a removable back for just such fishing excursions as this. Peter was far too excited to lean back against the rest as he let out his line. Jim put his line out on the side as he steered *Kitty Clyde's Sister* along the jetty.

The thrill of fishing from a moving boat always began here for Peter. The single motor purred. The propeller blade made deep-throated gurgling sounds as it rose to the surface of the water and dipped back in again with the rocking and plunging of the boat in the rolling swells. Peter slowly paid out line, watching his bait fish twirl and glide through the water. Soon the bait dropped out of sight.

Peter fixed his gaze on the spot where his line entered the water. He watched until his line stretched out just far enough behind the boat. He knew that from where the line entered the water, the heavy weight attached would carry his bait twenty or thirty feet below the watery trail left by *Kitty Clyde's Sister*.

Thus he sat, watching and waiting. He held his rod tip up and kept one hand on the reel handle. He was ready for a tug, a nibble, or maybe even a solid strike. Glancing over his shoulder, Peter saw that his father was settled into the day's fishing also. The two friends smiled broadly at each other.

Kitty Clyde's Sister shared the bay with many other boats that day—so many that Jim had to be careful in making his turns not to cross too closely behind another boat with trolling lines out. That first pass by the jetty was without results. It was early yet.

Other boats around the bay were having success. Anglers were in various postures of fishing activity. Here a man stood hauling on a bended rod while a fellow nearby held a big net in readiness. There a woman was reeling and pulling as her husband coached and encouraged her in the fight. Occupants of boats nearby watched anxiously to see the fish landed, cheering every successful angler.

When a party of fishermen saw another angler hook a fish, shouts went up. "Fish on! Hookup!" Then, anybody nearby who had a line out reeled it in immediately. That way there was no danger that the fish might tangle two lines together and effect its escape.

All the while clouds of squawking seagulls swarmed above the watery scene. Anglers had to be careful or these hungry scavengers would snatch the bait as it was let out behind the boat. It was not unusual on days like this to see some luckless bird flopping and struggling about in the water at the end of an annoyed fisherman's

December King

line. When released, these less-than-intelligent creatures simply ruffled their feathers (as though smoothing their dignity) and went right back to chasing baited hooks.

Flying higher with less flurry and more dignity were the pelicans. They seemed to disdain the seagulls with their frantic and undiscriminating fishing habits. The grace and poise of the pelicans as they soared high overhead outclassed the amateurish practices of the gulls. They went about their task quietly, their concentration on the water far below. Seldom flapping, the sac-beaked birds relied heavily on air currents to keep them aloft. Quickly adjusting their wings to catch the shifting wind, they were the picture of combined flying and fishing skill. With so many salmon in the bay chasing schools of food fish to the surface, the pelicans had more than enough to eat.

Peter was gazing at all this activity around him when he heard a commotion behind him. His father shouted, "Hey!" As he shouted, the water broke fifty feet behind *Kitty Clyde's Sister*. A large salmon leaped into the air, the sunlight gleaming on his silver sides. Jim gave a mighty pull with his rod and set the hook. The fight was on.

The fish was a silver salmon—not a Chinook—but it was quite large. By the time Jim got the fish to the side of the boat where Peter could gaff it, a good ten minutes had passed. A cheer went up from the boats nearby as Jim helped Peter lift the big silver into the boat.

"Wow, Dad, that's some fish!" Peter exclaimed with glee.

"At least Mother will let us come home now," his father replied through a grin.

The big silver salmon looked to be at least as large as the one that Peter had caught on their last fishing trip. Peter hoped that this one would weigh in at thirty pounds or more. That way his dad would get his picture taken at the "Big Fish" sign. Peter would be proud to see his father's picture on the board in the cannery whenever he went in.

Jim knew that his son was hoping to get his own picture with a

"Big Fish" up on the board. After he baited both lines with fresh anchovies, he told Peter, "Get your bait in the water, Son. It's your turn this time."

Peter complied gladly, saying with determination, "I'm ready."

Two more passes were made along the rock jetty. The jetty was lined with fishermen today. Those who did not own and could not rent boats found this to be the next best way to fish. By casting far out and reeling in, they had a good chance of hooking one of the many fish in the bay.

As *Kitty Clyde's Sister* cruised by slowly now, Jim noticed one of the shore fishermen who was battling a salmon. "That's one of the fellows who wanted to rent a boat this morning, Peter," he said.

They were both pleased to see that this man had not come up empty-handed after not being able to rent a boat. They whooped and hollered when he landed his fish. The man saw them and waved with a big grin on his face.

Several fish were being caught all around the bay. Peter did not lose hope, even though he had not yet had a strike. On the third pass opposite the jetty, Peter was staring intently at his line where it entered the water. The boat was moving slowly, and Peter could just see a small *V* ripple the surface of the water as his line passed through it. It was afternoon now.

"Whoa!" Peter shouted. He had felt a mighty tug. He let out line. Then he waited, not daring to breathe. Nothing. Finally, he had to reset his reel (if he let out too much line, he ran the risk of getting snagged). What a disappointment! He had missed what might prove to be his only opportunity to catch a fish for the day.

Jim said, "Pull your line in and check your bait. You may have lost it."

Peter complied. He reeled in his line, feeling disgusted at his missed chance.

"Wham!" The rod plunged straight down and smacked the brass rail on the back of the boat. Jim cut the motor immediately. He thought that Peter was snagged. Peter's reel whirred madly as the line went singing out. *Kitty Clyde's Sister* slowed and came to a stop. The line was still paying out.

"You've got one, Son! Hold your pole up!" Jim shouted.

"I can't!" shrieked Peter.

Try as he would to pull his pole up from the side of the boat, Peter couldn't get it off the rail. Indeed, it was all that he could do to hold on and keep from losing his whole rig over the back of the boat.

"Brace your feet on the rail!" Jim coached.

Peter got his feet up. He was almost pulled from his seat as he did so. The line was going out at an incredible rate. It never slowed. There was only two hundred yards of line on the reel. If Peter could not slow this fish down, it would take every foot.

With a mighty effort, feet braced and back against the rest, Peter heaved on his pole. He did it! He got the tip of his pole up! Now the fish would have to fight the flexible rod. Maybe that would tire him out.

The line kept stripping off. Peter could see the blue of the yarn which his dad had helped him to put on the reel for a soft backing under the forty-pound line. The line was clear monofilament. There couldn't be more than a few yards left if the backing showed through. Peter's heart almost stopped. "Dad!" he cried out frantically. But his father didn't hear him.

Jim had seen the predicament that Peter was in. Just as Peter cried out, he started both motors and gave them full power in reverse. *Kitty Clyde's Sister* responded quickly. Peter was about to give up hope when the boat got up speed, and the line stopped going out. Peter began to reel furiously. He gasped for breath as he worked. In the early moments of the fight, he had almost forgotten to breathe.

Jim kept his eyes on the line and backed straight toward it. For a full minute they did this. Then Jim slowed the motors. By now every fisherman in the area had his line out of the water. Whoops and shouts went up all around. Everyone could see that this was a mighty fighting fish. Some speculated that it was a ray or a shark (sharks sometimes ventured into the saltwater bay in search of food). Out of courtesy for the young boy with a hook-up, the boats pushed out away from *Kitty Clyde's Sister* to give him plenty of room for playing his fish. Neither Peter nor his dad noticed this courtesy. They were intent on the battle at hand.

When Jim slowed the boat, Peter was still reeling. Now Jim stopped the motors, unwilling to risk cutting the line with the propellers. This made Peter anxious. He had regained precious little line. He figured that he only had fifty yards or so on the reel. "Don't worry, Son. We can start her up again if it runs," Jim said reassuringly.

The fish was not running now. However, it was pulling with tremendous force. Peter kept reeling, but no line came in. The reel was set to slip when the strain was near the breaking point of the line. It was slipping now. The line was stretched tight. Droplets slid along the length above water. They glistened in the sun and made it easy to see which direction the fish was heading.

Until now the line had reached straight out behind *Kitty Clyde's Sister*. The tugging on the other end was constant. Peter thought that it felt like he was hooked on a submarine. His back began to ache. Sweat lined his brow. Jim spoke encouragement to Peter, telling him to hang in there. The line began to move in a wide circle away from the jetty. Peter had to turn to follow the big fish. He braced himself as best he could against the side of the boat. The fish was near the surface now. The line lay on top of the water far out from the boat.

Something broke the water at the end of the line. The big fish did not jump. He just swam steadily in a wide circle. "Is it a shark, Dad?" Peter asked when he saw the dark, pointed object slice through the water for an instant.

"Son, that was no dorsal fin," answered Jim from his vantage point. "That was the tail fin of a king salmon—the biggest tail fin I have ever seen!"

Peter's heart pounded with excitement. Chills shot up his spine to tingle on the back of his neck. "Really?" he asked breathlessly. Determination sprang up in his heart. "I am strong enough," he said to himself. Peter's awareness of the fatigue and the ache in his back faded. The glorious thrill of this great challenge filled him with new strength.

"If you get too tired, I'll hold your rod for a while, Son," Jim offered.

"I can do it!" Peter replied soberly.

Jim's heart warmed with pride as he watched his son putting forth such a valiant effort in the fierce struggle. He would do all that he could to help his son catch this fish.

Jim started the motors again. The great fish was directly opposite the side of the boat now. Peter was still unable to gain an inch as his quarry hung hard against the pull of the rod. Jim angled *Kitty Clyde's Sister* toward the forward path of the fish, moving slowly in that direction. Peter was able to reel in more line. Slowly he took it in, keeping it tight against the pulling of the great fish.

Suddenly, the pulling stopped. Peter was frantic. He reeled with all of his might. Had the big Chinook broken loose? Jim cut the motors. "Smack!" went the pole against the rail. "Zzzzzzz," screamed the line. The giant fish had turned toward the boat, and now it was sounding. Straight for the bottom it dived, tearing off as much line as it wanted.

Peter struggled to raise his pole once again. The big fish had earned his respect. Peter only hoped that his opponent could not feel how weary he was becoming from the fight. Could the great fish read from the strain on the line that it was requiring more and more effort on Peter's part to hamper its movements? With a terrific heave, Peter managed to raise the rod. The line slowed and then stopped running out. The monster had reached bottom.

A new scene developed. As Peter struggled to hold his pole up over the side of the boat, the great fish swam effortlessly in a narrow circle relying on its weight to keep its depth. The line traced small loops on the water's surface as the salmon swam. For fully twenty minutes this went on. Jim brought Peter a drink of water. He held the cup to his son's lips and helped him drink. Then he rubbed Peter's shoulders. He knew that they must ache terribly by now. All the while, Jim spoke encouragement.

Things took a turn for the worse. The circles got wider and then stopped. The line snaked inward toward the side of the boat. The fish kept its depth. Peter didn't dare lean over the side, but Jim watched as the line came right up to the side of the boat. The reel started to sing.

"He's moving under the boat!" Jim announced with concern. Springing quickly to the rear of *Kitty Clyde's Sister,* he tilted the outboard motors, bringing the propellers up out of the water—first one, then the other. There was only one chance to keep from losing this fish and Jim knew it. "Son, you are going to have to get around the boat or he will cut the line on the bottom," he said in an urgent tone.

Peter could see that what his father said was true. He wondered if he could do it though. He stood up. The strain on his back and legs was tremendous. Following his father's instructions, he stuck his pole tip into the water to clear the bottom of the boat. The line was still paying out. A quick surge of the fish's massive tail fin would snatch the rod from Peter's hands in this precarious position. Peter mustered all of his strength. Slowly, and only with the fiercest effort, he forced the rod around the corner of the boat then out and around the uplifted motors. He had done it! Flopping down on the seat, Peter puffed and puffed, trying to catch his breath. Still the line went out.

The steady strain on his pole was beginning to make every muscle in Peter's young body ache. How much longer could he hold out? Better than an hour had passed already, and the big fish was still swimming away from the boat. The glory of the contest was fading. This adventure was proving to be more than a match for the skill and equipment at Peter's disposal. With those advantages gone, the contest was reduced to a simple test of strength. At that moment,

Peter was seriously doubting that his strength was adequate for the test. Reluctantly, he was about to call on his father for help when his reel stopped turning.

Here was an unexpected advantage for Peter. His line stretched out from the side of *Kitty Clyde's Sister* directly toward the jetty. The noble Chinook had committed a grave error. It was now contained between the boat and the jetty.

A crowd of fishermen lined the jetty. They were all anxiously watching this most unusual battle (anyone who has ever fished for salmon knows the feeling of respect that these great fish generate in those who pursue them). Out of that respect, there was a common bond between the salmon fishermen on shore and Peter. When they saw this young boy in a struggle with a big fish, they became almost as involved as they would have been were they holding the twitching rod. Peter was unaware of the audience gathered to watch his fight.

Suddenly there was a roar from the shoreline. The crowd had seen something awesome. The great fish, finding its path blocked by the jetty, had risen quickly to the surface. Its momentum carried the giant body halfway out of the water. So broad was the front half that the spectators could scarcely believe their eyes when the Chinook broke water barely ten feet from shore.

Among those wide-eyed spectators was one who felt mixed emotions. Johnny Mark had not been invited by his father to go fishing on this big day. All alone he had made his way out onto the jetty to try and make good his boast that he would catch the biggest fish that year. Now he stood astonished by the size of the salmon before him. It was Peter's fish. At least, it would be if he could land the gigantic Chinook.

Johnny Mark was in a dilemma. On the one hand, he was caught up in the cheering and rooting for a fellow fisherman. On the other hand, the boy who was the object of his jealousy was about to catch what would certainly be the biggest fish of the day. This new boy who was a threat to his importance at school was about to outfish him.

Peter did not see Johnny. His attention was completely occupied by the struggle for mastery over the formidable fish. No words could describe the agony that Peter felt as he fought to take in line. His arms were weak. His shoulders and back were sore. His hands wanted to let go. Still he fought on.

Several minutes passed without a change. Peter reeled, and the reel slipped. He was unable to gain a foot. The big fish swam back and forth, as though searching for a way around the jetty. Then, almost imperceptibly, the line began to come in. Peter reeled steadily. The salmon pulled steadily. The line came in by inches. The Chinook began to make its turns toward the boat instead of away from it. On these occasions, Peter was able to reel in three or four feet of line. The great fish was tiring.

Peter was encouraged. He found new strength in the thought that he was gaining the upper hand. Soon the fish was only fifty yards out. It could not be seen yet, but it was getting closer. Peter began to pump his rod up and down as he reeled. Up, and then reel as it went down. Up again, and reel as it went down. It was working. Soon he would see his fish. Twice Peter got the giant creature within twenty yards. Each time a frantic flip of the king's great tail fin sent it surging away. Yards of line went streaking out. Each time it seemed an impossible chore to regain that line, but somehow Peter managed. He was on his feet now, lifting the rod with all his might.

Finally, when every ounce of his strength seemed to be gone, Peter saw his quarry. A tremendous shadowy form heaved into view deep below. Then it disappeared under the boat. Peter's mouth hung open. When he saw that shadow, his knees buckled. He caught himself and regained his composure. "Did you see that?" he gasped.

"He's huge!" Jim exclaimed, incredulously. Jim stood ready with the gaff hook as Peter renewed his effort.

Again the monster Chinook loomed into view. This time it was only ten feet down. Peter could see the fins and the giant tail of the fish. He kept a steady pressure on the rod now, trying not to startle

December King

the fish. Back and forth the salmon swam. One minute it was in view, the next it was under the boat. When next they saw it, Peter had managed to raise it to within five feet of the surface. Now they could see its mouth opening and closing. The gill slits alongside the king's head heaved with fatigue.

Peter saw that one of his two hooks was hanging free. Only one hook held this mighty fish. What if his father missed with the gaff and startled the giant? Peter knew that he could not withstand another furious run by the king salmon. As it turned out, he did not have time to dwell on this horrible thought. This time, when the salmon slid into view, it was barely a foot from the watery surface.

"Lift your rod steadily with all your might the next time he comes out from under the boat, Peter," Jim said. "Here he comes!"

Peter gathered what strength he had left and did as his father said.

Like lightning Jim struck the fish with the gaff. The hook sunk deep. The Chinook thrashed furiously, and its sheer weight almost wrenched the gaff handle from Jim's hands. After the valiant effort put forth by his son, Jim was not about to lose this fish now. He clenched his teeth and gave a mighty heave. Up, up, and over the rail.

Peter scrambled to get out of the way of the flopping giant. Finally, the exhausted but victorious fisherman dropped to his seat drained of every last scrap of strength. The conquered king quit flopping and lay still.

What a cheer went up! Fishermen everywhere were yelling, clapping, and whistling. In the final moments of the battle, the surrounding boats had closed in to see the fish landed. Now they formed a horseshoe from the jetty, all the way around *Kitty Clyde's Sister,* and back to the jetty.

Peter was embarrassed when his dad made him stand up to take a bow. Such an ovation from so many fishermen would embarrass most young boys. Jim tried to hold the big Chinook up for everyone to see. Try as he would, he couldn't get the tail off the deck as he lifted the fish with one hand in each gill slit.

On the jetty Johnny Mark stood cheering. He had forgotten his jealousy of Peter in the excitement of the moment. He was cheering for a fellow fisherman who had won a great victory against a formidable foe. Peter glanced up and saw Johnny. This remarkable display of support by the boy who had been the scourge of his school days caused Peter no little wonder.

The ride back to the docks was like heaven for Peter. He had done it! This fish had to be the biggest of the day. Peter couldn't stop staring at the mammoth Chinook. It looked like the biggest fish in the world. It was easily twice as large as the one his father had caught.

Jim Miles stood erect at the wheel of *Kitty Clyde's Sister*. His chest was puffed up with pride for his young son. He laughed and smiled broadly as he waved acknowledgment to the shouts of congratulations from boats along the way. Peter was still weary and a little bit dazed. He sat quietly. A warm glow radiated through his body. There was a satisfied smile on his face.

Somehow word had reached the docks ahead of the successful fishermen. A crowd had gathered. Nancy and Anne were there waiting. Nancy was excited. Little Anne did not understand what all the commotion was about, but she could feel the excitement in the crowd of curious onlookers gathered around her. It made her giggle.

A man from the local newspaper, carrying a camera, arrived at the scene just as *Kitty Clyde's Sister* slipped alongside the dock. The crowd let out a breathless "Wow" of amazement when Jim heaved the great Chinook onto the dock with the help of a big, strong fellow in the crowd. The newspaperman took several pictures of the fish and Peter. He asked Jim all about the battle to catch the fish, who he was, what his boy's name was, and many other details. He said that this was going to make all the papers for miles around. "This is big news," he said.

Meanwhile Nancy hugged Peter and smiled with pride as the crowd of onlookers slapped him on the back and thoroughly congratulated him. Peter was speechless in the face of all this attention. He was a little bit embarrassed by all the fuss.

When they finally got the mighty king salmon over to the cannery for the moment that he had longed for—the picture at the "Big Fish" sign—Peter was feeling so humble that he could only manage a shy smile. Nevertheless, he knew that he would never forget that moment. His greatest dream had come true.

11
Home Sweet Home

Sunday was a wonderful day. The local paper carried a big article on the front page with a picture of Peter and his Chinook at the "Big Fish" sign. The caption read, "Local boy catches granddaddy Chinook weighing sixty pounds!" The article accompanying the picture said, "Peter and his family are new residents at the river. His father, Jim Miles, owns and operates Best Place for Miles, a boat-rental shop at the mouth of the river." Jim said that it was terrific advertising for the business.

All day Peter relived the drama of his big battle of the day before. Now that it was all over, the pain and the hardship dimmed in the light of his glorious victory. That evening brought two surprises.

First, Bruce Bobo stopped by to announce that he had spoken with Chautauqua. All of Peter's friends upriver were overjoyed when they read the account of his victory in the newspaper. Aunt Molly told Chautauqua that he must come down Monday for supplies and to convey congratulations to the "mighty fisherman," as she put it. That was the good news. Chautauqua would be down to visit. Nancy said that she would insist that he stay the night.

The other surprise was Jim's doing. Unknown to Peter, his father had arranged with Jack Johnson at the cannery to have Peter's trophy fish stuffed and mounted for display in the family store. J.J. counted it an honor to be chosen for the task. Accordingly, he spent the whole day Sunday at the business of mounting the huge Chinook. He brought the finished product over to the Miles's house that evening. He was obviously quite proud of his masterpiece. He wouldn't even accept payment for the job. Jim tried very hard to make him take some money, but to no avail.

After J.J. had departed, as Peter gazed reverently at his prize salmon, Jim said, "Son, since Mr. Johnson refuses to accept payment for his work, I want you to have it. Consider it a fee for advertising. We'll hang your Chinook on the wall in the shop for our customers' amazement." With that he gave Peter twenty-five dollars.

Peter was shocked by this unexpected windfall. He was about to say that he couldn't take the money either when suddenly he thought of a use for the sum. "Thanks, Dad. Can I spend it any way I want?" he asked.

"It's your money, and you may do with it as you please," Jim replied.

That night, as Peter was getting ready for bed, he emptied the jar containing his fish-cleaning earnings onto his bed. With the twenty-five dollars that his father had given him, he had almost fifty dollars. Peter went to sleep with a smile on his face.

Monday morning found Peter in an unusual mood. Instead of being reluctant to go to school, he was calmly eager for whatever the day might bring. His good fortune had fortified him so that he was ready for any challenge.

The walk to school in the brisk December air was invigorating. Peter looked at the water of the bay with a new feeling of kinship as he crossed the bridge. He truly felt that he belonged in this river country. Out on the water, he had faced a tremendous test. It was almost as though the river had thrown its biggest challenge at him, and he had mastered it. What could possibly defeat him now?

School was a totally different experience that day. Peter's classmates greeted him with a cheer as he entered the room. Before Mrs. Pomroy could calm everyone down to start the class, each student had to shake Peter's hand. They all wanted to know what it was like to catch such a big fish. All, except Johnny Mark that is.

While Peter recounted the struggle of his ordeal with the great

Chinook to his eager audience, Johnny sat quietly at his desk in the back of the room. Peter didn't notice, as he happily answered the many questions. He was too busy reliving the thrill of his wonderful experience with his truly friendly classmates.

By lunchtime everyone was ready to hear the whole story all over again. Peter finally became weary of being the center of attention. Mrs. Pomroy, in her wisdom, called him up to her desk when she saw that the other students were wearing him out with all their avid attention. The cold wind blowing outside dictated that everyone remain inside that day. Mrs. Pomroy asked Peter to help her carry some extra books to the office for an excuse to talk with him alone.

When they were in the office, the kindly teacher took Peter aside and said, "I wanted to congratulate you too. That was a wonderful thrill for you, wasn't it?"

"Yes, it was," Peter replied humbly.

Then she continued. "I know that you have not had an easy time getting adjusted here at school these past weeks, Peter. Johnny Mark has been very hard on you. He has caused the others to be less than friendly also. I have admired your strength in the face of such rejection. It takes character to refrain from returning unkindness for unkindness."

Peter started to say something, but Mrs. Pomroy held up her hand and said, "I simply want you to keep up the good work. And I think that you are mature enough to understand what I am going to tell you."

She then explained to Peter why Johnny Mark regarded him with such hostility. She told him about the difficult conditions in Johnny's home. Then she asked him to promise to keep all that she had said to himself. Peter readily agreed.

When school let out, Peter was deep in thought. He soberly acknowledged his classmates' good-byes as they filed out the door to go home. Then as Mrs. Pomroy looked on with a secret smile, Peter approached Johnny Mark. Johnny was solemnly collecting his

Home Sweet Home

things together for the walk home. Peter hesitated. Then he said, "I saw you on the jetty, Saturday."

"Yeah, so what," was the sullen reply.

"Did you have any luck?" Peter asked undaunted.

"I didn't catch a thing," said Johnny, "but I would have if I'd 'a' had a boat."

"Would you like to go out on *Kitty Clyde's Sister* with me and my dad next weekend?" Peter offered. Peter knew that his father would understand and would gladly take them out when he heard the whole story.

Johnny Mark said nothing.

"If the weather's good, of course," Peter added, nonchalantly.

"Yeah, sure, if the weather's good, it would be all right," Johnny answered in kind.

"Great. See ya," Peter concluded cheerfully. Then, as he turned to leave the room, Johnny said after him, "Bet I catch the biggest fish."

"I hope you do," Peter answered with a smile.

Johnny was convicted. "Couldn't be as big as your king, though," he said.

From that conversation, it was plain to Peter that God (or the Great Spirit as he sometimes called him now) had allowed the situation with Johnny Mark to develop so that he, Peter, might experience loneliness. Now having been schooled in the piteous depths of despair that afflict those who are lonely, Peter found it remarkably easy to understand Johnny Mark and to put up with his ill temper. Quite obviously this was an answer to his prayer. From his loneliness at school, Peter had learned compassion for the lonely.

Peter didn't go straight home from school. He had permission from his parents to run an errand. When he finally did get home, Chautauqua was there.

Peter was carrying a package besides his schoolbooks. He said hello to Chautauqua and then excused himself saying, "I'll be right back. I've got to put my stuff away in my room." He hurried upstairs. Jim and Nancy both thought that this was strange behavior for their son. He had been looking forward to Chautauqua's visit with such excitement.

When Peter came back downstairs, he apologized for running off. Then he shook Chautauqua's hand warmly, welcoming his friend to his home. "I'm glad you could come to my home, Chautauqua. You have already met my parents, I see."

"Yes, my brother, we have introduced ourselves. You have a fine home and a good family. Your little sister thinks that I am funny to look at," the big Indian said with a grin. Anne was peeking out from behind Nancy's dress and giggling. It was obvious that she was being very shy.

Peter took great delight in showing his good friend around the docks and the shop. In the shop, Chautauqua admired Peter's salmon which hung on the wall. When he had gazed at the majestic fish for quite some time, he said to Peter, "You have had an unusual experience, my brother. It was no easy task landing that fish. You have learned a great lesson from this mighty Chinook I would guess. From now on I think that I will call you 'Chinook.' This will remind you of your great fortune, and it will symbolize the kinship that we feel for each other."

Peter marveled at how this wise man could say so much with so few words. He smiled warmly at his Indian friend.

After they had eaten, Nancy invited Chautauqua to spend the night with them. He accepted. Peter excused himself again. "I'll be right back," he said and bounded up the stairs to his room.

Jim and Chautauqua built up the fire in the living room. They were just sitting down to enjoy the warmth when Peter returned. "These are for you if they fit and you want them," he said as he handed a pair of beautiful black cowboy boots to Chautauqua. They were stitched with an intricate design and shone so that you could see the fire in the fireplace reflecting in their luster.

The boots had cost Peter forty dollars, and it was worth every penny to see the look of surprise and pleasure on Chautauqua's face.

Home Sweet Home

Jim smiled with admiration too. So that was why Peter had been so secretive. Nancy came in with hot chocolate and cookies just in time to see the presentation.

Chautauqua was silent. He looked at Peter with a smile so warm that the fire in the fireplace could not compete. He tried the boots on, and they fit.

Peter said, "I got the same size that Dad wears. The man at the store said that you can exchange them if they don't fit."

"They make my feet as happy as your friendship makes me, Chinook," replied Chautauqua.

The evening was one of laughter and good feelings as Chautauqua told fascinating stories of the river country and his ancestors. He invited Peter to go snowshoeing with him when the snows came. Peter accepted the invitation wholeheartedly. He thought for a moment, and then he asked if he might bring a friend along. "Johnny Mark could learn a lot from my friend Chautauqua," he reasoned to himself.

As the evening was drawing to an end, Peter looked up at the mantel over the fireplace. "Home Sweet Home" had a new and wonderful meaning. Later, when all had said good-night, Peter knelt by his bed.

"God, Great Spirit, You have shown me your purpose for my unhappiness of the past. Now I thank you for the happiness of the present, and I promise that I will look to you for purpose in the future."